LONGING FOR CERTAINTY

LONGING FOR CERTAINTY

REFLECTIONS ON THE BUDDHIST LIFE

Bhikkhu Nyanasobhano

Wisdom Publications
Boston

Wisdom Publications
199 Elm Street
Somerville MA 02214 USA
www.wisdompubs.org

Library of Congress Cataloging-in-Publication Data

Nyanasobhano, Bhikkhu
  Longing for certainty : reflections on the
Buddhist life / Bhikkhu Nyanasobhano.
    p. cm.
    ISBN 0-86171-338-9 (alk. paper)
    1. Spiritual life—Buddhism. 2. Buddhism—
Doctrines. I. Title.
BQ4302.N94 2002
294.3/42041-dc21   2002151891

First Edition
08 07 06 05 04 03
6   5   4   3   2   1

Cover design by Roger Dormann
Interior design by Stephanie Doyle

Wisdom Publications' books are printed on acid-free
paper and meet the guidelines for permanence and
durability set by the Council of Library Resources.

Printed in the United States of America

Contents

PREFACE

T he essays in this book explore the teachings of the Buddha from the standpoint of the *Theravāda,* the "doctrine of the elders." These teachings have come down to us in words, and it is through attention to words that we get our first understanding of how the Buddha viewed the world and how he advised his followers to practice in order to achieve happiness. But words too often remain theoretical for us, not moving us to action, unless we can find their concrete counterparts in our daily lives. One aim of this book, then, is to suggest how to look upon the scenes that surround us, how to find useful illustrations of Buddhist principles in our own immediate experience.

As strange and confusing as this human world is, it holds precious and obtainable truth. Sights, sounds, smells, and all kinds of sensory events blossom in endless profusion; mental and physical processes run on; actions produce results large and small. If we perceive these things with mindfulness and notice how they exemplify the teachings of the Buddha we can find the motivation and the means for a worthier life.

This book also aims to present Buddhism as a system of belief and practice founded upon the Buddha's understanding of how causes accumulate to bring about both joy and misery. When we explore with basic principles in mind we will be able to appreciate that this world, though shaken so by suffering, goes on as it does in a conditioned, lawful way, and that if we act according to noble standards—if we supply good conditions—we will be able to break up suffering and attain to peace.

The truths discovered by the Buddha are vast and wonderful. These essays only try to indicate some entryways to adventure. The world is rich enough with signs for seekers who will look around alertly.

Buddhist technical terms are given here in their Pali forms. The quotations from the Pali Canon are edited excerpts of translations published by Wisdom Publications and by the Buddhist Publication Society of Kandy, Sri Lanka. I have also made use of the *Buddha Jayanti Tripitaka Series* edition of the Pali Canon, published by the Sri Lanka Tripitaka Project.

1
ICE AND HOPE

It is one of those rare winter days that give rise to hope—a quiet, blue afternoon with the sun dazzling on thin snow. We are alone out here in the stillness of the hollow below the farms, wandering among big trees beside a creek, with no particular goal to excite us, no urgent duties, and for once no yammering misgivings to turn us back. We are roaming at will through this piece of woods, crossing the tracks of other creatures in a long excursion to who knows where. The snow lies on the hillsides shining and melting a little, and the creek runs brilliantly between edges of ice. How surprising, how amazing that we who long shrank stupefied under winter now expand so thoughtlessly at this least thaw and burn our hoarded energies in these unblossoming woods. What is to be gained from this whimsical exercise? What is this strange human hope that sets us walking and leads away from warmth and merriment into this out-of-the-way, sunny desolation?

As we walk through the brambles and broken weed-stalks, getting farther from our usual preoccupations, something stirs like a fragrance from that childish past when we marveled without words or comprehension at the splendid, startling, echoing world. It is a readiness, perhaps, and a wish to go on toward a rightful destiny where doubt and fear will fall away. How long has this readiness slept in the snow, crushed by habit, nearly extinguished? Now we feel it again here in the snowy hollow where the winter is being cut down by the liquid creek and by our own impetuous footsteps, our own eagerness for action. In the cold, bright air our senses seem keener, catching small lights and motions in nature, as if we were looking for signs of a reality long suspected but never quite attained. We are encouraged even at this anticipation. For all the deadening years, for all the strife and self-importance, for all the error and grief of adulthood, still this implausible longing, this childish hope, enlivens us once again.

On either side the forest mounts steeply, broken here and there by ledges of gray limestone. Now in the light and silence it all seems perfectly abandoned, raw, and desolate, yet beautiful or something more than beautiful. There is a feeling of impending, epochal change, as if spring were about to happen and all the snow were soon to melt and show us an unimagined landscape. For a moment we pause, hearing our own breathing and looking around slowly on this enigmatic afternoon with the sun low but warm enough and the shadows of trees blue and vague on coarse snow. Maybe the abandoned valley reflects a possibility in us, a theoretical, unknown season; but if so we still lack the crucial understanding with which to bring it on, and while our breath holds out we must keep wandering with a ready mind.

We pass through withered undergrowth along the bank of the creek, where the ice gleams wetly and the channel of free water shows rippling trees and skies. Briars and dead wood block our way, but as we have left the faint path long before, we are not much bothered and only walk a little more deliberately, detouring where we must, turning, hopping, striding, adapting ourselves to the land. We have not expected a trail, in any case, and we derive a kind of gladness in making this roundabout tour whose goal is not efficiency but a gracefulness of mind as much as of body. Though the briars do not spare us and the silent trees do not welcome us or offer any fruit, yet we adapt, bend with the silent change in all these things, and use our eyes and ears to catch what is happening. There is, for the moment, a fitness just in watching and listening and walking with due care; and we wonder whether with energetic contemplation we could out-walk words entirely, leave them behind, and meet the world unencumbered.

We notice that we have not yet arrived at a perfect indifference to comfort, for we are keeping to the sunlit part of the hollow and feel no temptation to cross the creek to the shadowed, colder side. The tranquil air and the brilliant sun are keeping us cheerful after so much dreary winter, and this cheerfulness is a welcome sensation—so let us go on without worry and devote ourselves more fully to this quiet business of observing and keeping our balance. The snow, we see, has lost its uniformity and freshness. Now it is partly melted and mottled and sprinkled with pine needles, shriveled leaves, stems, and sticks. Indistinct footprints of animals run over the rough surface, and we press down our own tracks among them, reflecting on this impermanent history of the day. Stamp how we will, the snow takes all marks and melts away. Even the trees and the rocks seem oddly impermanent, now that we look: there are many rotten stumps and haggard standing trunks and fallen dead branches all around; and the jutting limestone, when we walk over to inspect it, is a puzzle of cracks and divisions. Even the magnificent sky is defaced by faint shreds of cloud. We find, more and more, not perfection but slow upheaval, an ever-aging panorama of transient, crumbling, recombining things.

Now we turn away, just at a whim, and wander up a little tributary stream that trickles out of the hillside. Here we come upon a half-frozen pool below a face of rock bulging with icicles. In other seasons this must be a splashing, enchanting little waterfall, but now the water is held back and transformed into strange, white, glistening stone, frozen in layer upon layer. It drips into the pool irregularly; but there is a great mass of ice hanging off the rock and we cannot tell whether this slow thawing will much diminish it or whether the water continually seeping and draining out of the earth will make it grow still greater in the night to come.

We shuffle around the pool, admiring the desolate beauty—if that is what it is—and listening to the splatter of water-drops and squinting into the icicles. The snow at our feet here has melted back to reveal a soggy, earth-colored mat of leaves with a few still-green tufts of grass. We know—in a distant, irrelevant way—that the spring heat will soon draw up a new generation of greenery and display to the wanderer a livelier, more accommodating scene; but what power do we have over that, we who live now and want comfort now? What do we really understand of the clash or blend of elements that makes possible the frozen waterfall? As for our own troubled hearts—what do we understand of how afflictions come and go? Certainly we respond by instinct to these tones struck by nature, but for all the resounding elation or gloom, we remain dependent, never fully knowing and never transcending the pageant of ceaseless change.

The ice has not spilled over the rough rock ledges for anybody's good or pleasure, as far as we can tell. It simply swells in the silent hollow, arising out of unknown laws; and if we are like most sightseers we will admire it for a minute and maybe carry away a small sensation of awe or refreshment. Our experience will be briefly enriched, that is all. But what if, instead, we make our minds glide more intently over these surfaces, outlasting our casual curiosity? Let us perceive beauty—or whatever we choose to call these austere flourishes of winter—but let us think as well, taking from our observation, if we can, the matter for more durable reflection.

What shall we make of the frozen waterfall? Is it not a happy chance that has brought us, strangely hopeful, here to see it, outside the talkative world in the sunlit, silent theatre of the woods? We might regard the ice as a symbol of impermanence, or of the secret creativity of nature, or of some stern principle beneath the surface of existence, or of the right resolve too long frozen within us—but symbol or not, the frozen water-fall is certainly an outlandish presence that reminds us how little we have really explored, how seldom we have crossed habit into freer territory. If this afternoon we have wandered out to a country of contemplation, that is good; but will we ever get beyond mere miles, and beyond the limits of dreaming, to some brave and wakeful truth at last? The mechanical sea-sons around us, which we have long taken for granted, are capable, we see, of extraordinary creations; so what fine work might a conscious human being do? Although we have for so many years supposed that our lives can only flow on in one desultory, unsatisfying way, perhaps it is our own resignation or stubborn error that keeps the stream in its muddy channel. Desiring and hoping alone will surely not suffice to alter the current (for we have desired and hoped for ages). Some strong, coherent knowledge is what we need.

Now we wait uncomfortably, worrying that soon we are going to get cold and that soon we are going to feel reasons to shrug and hurry back to our routines. The sunlight, even now, is receding up the hill, leaving the waterfall in shadow. We wonder whether the dripping icicles will now freeze again and the whole strange construction will be preserved another night, or whether the definitive change in season has indeed come and the phase of solidity will end. And would that be good or bad? We hardly know; and anyway the crystalline waterfall keeps turning our wondering back upon ourselves. We have no certainty of a season to thaw our coldness. Nothing guarantees us the elimination of our burdens or the preservation of our delights. No fate that we know of ensures our betterment. From time to time, as today, a rare inspiration startles us, but we do not know where it comes from and we have no way to build upon it. There will be more change, certainly, as always, and in our ignorance of the laws of change how can we expect a perpetual happiness? Where is there a way out of ignorance?

Hope has risen in us as we have walked and watched and let the moving scenes go by, and we fear now that it will simply fall away when not sustained, not given substance by intelligent action—just another mood that briefly animates us and departs, as a breeze agitates grass but leaves behind no power. Surely there are laws, conditions, or causes here yet undiscovered by us, the knowledge of which would give us strength; but how shall we find them? After this lifetime of wandering and improvising we are still shivering inside our homemade philosophies—so ragged after so much knitting! Even if we think ourselves sensitive and capable, even if we are wishing for the good and would undertake some worthy work, still we lack the right means, the direction, the path through the mortal wilderness. Where is the firm ground to hold us up? Where is the spring breeze to urge us along?

In this hollow below the stark sky and the high, thin branches of the trees, we find ourselves deprived of distractions, and it seems right that at least we meet directly the central problem of our ignorance. If we had just a start, we think, just a promising goal, we might have a chance for progress into knowledge. Perhaps, then, it is time to set down our pride and admit our confusion (no one will laugh at us out in this fair solitude) and look for help in the example of an earlier wanderer. We can read footprints that time has not melted. If we cannot at once break out of the circle of our hungry thoughts, we can listen to a teacher who has gone further. We can remember what once surprised our browsing minds and bring it here, away from the libraries, out of the realm of theory, and try it against the actual winter.

It is not words, at first, that now comes to our aid, but the memory or imagination of a human figure—a man we have never seen in this life but yet, from legend, art, or intuition, we can almost picture. Maybe we have many times daydreamed back through centuries to imagine that majestic figure sitting immobile in the forest, or walking with slow, silent grace, or speaking, in absolute serenity, of solemn and wondrous matters. We envision the Buddha, the Enlightened One, the great teacher whose life and doctrine have so marked history that we today, perhaps even before we knew much of the doctrine he taught, have felt undeniable attraction. Some ideas, notions, wisps of teaching have floated through our minds; we have passed, in museums or in temples, tranquil images of the Buddha; we have thought wistfully of enlightenment and wondered whether we could ever reach it. We retain the still vague but lasting picture of a sage who knew the world through and through and had compassion for all living beings, a man perfected and at peace.

The fact that the Buddha was a mortal human being and not a god or a supernatural being of any kind interests us more, for it suggests that his splendid deliverance from ignorance and suffering was not the automatic fulfillment of a unique nature but rather something built, earned, and achieved, something attained by human effort in this thorny world. Once he was simply a young man alive and thinking amid the storms of birth and death; and later, after great striving, he overcame the ancient impediments to reach perfect enlightenment. By earnest investigation and effort the Buddha discovered the path to the ending of suffering and followed it all the way; then he taught, sharing his knowledge with the world. Might we then set foot on this path and follow it ourselves, for our own benefit? Is such a thing possible? We have heard, in his recorded words, that it is.

That, and whatever else we might have learned of Buddhist doctrine, was back in closed rooms—a matter to stimulate the mind, to aid philosophy—but have we ever till now, marching and surviving under the brilliant cold sky, fully breathed in the words and matched their meaning to what we see and hear and sense? The Buddha taught that all conditioned things—all objects, thoughts, and situations—are impermanent. They rise and fall, appear and vanish. Desired or undesired, they inevitably change and pass away. Well then, is this true? Let us look around us. Will this welcome sun stand ever burning just so? Will this snow last out the year or the week? How long does a single breath of ours float visible before us? What about the tall young trees, standing amid the old wreckage of their kind? We see a momentary sky, whose pure blue is now more and more streaked with cloud. We notice our melting footprints in the slush. We see the fractured limestone in the side of the hill. We see the shimmering stream and the ice that grows and melts. And in us, through us, gushes the current of feelings and intentions, too fast to hold onto. Where is there permanence?

If even rock—divided by ice, dissolved by rain—cannot hold together, if everything we can detect is on the move in some way, lapsing helplessly into some other form, on what foundation can we possibly base our happiness? What pleasure or consolation can we trust? Must all our satisfactions end in sad regret? That is how it seems now in this universe of hectic change. We stand rocking uneasily, hands in pockets, unable to reconcile the remembered smile of the Buddha with the unrest he saw and declared. For this is surely an unsatisfactory situation. Stone itself is crumbling in the depths of the hollow, while we have been trusting to airy sensations for our safety—to tastes, sights, sounds, and ideas with no more substance than blown ashes. Sorrows encroach on our dreams and we see no remedy but to dodge faster into diversions. In the pains of the moment, and under the shadow of imminent miseries, we hasten to entertainments, attributing to them a spiritual balm they do not have. Overloaded with worry, we take on a fresh load of excitement; but repeated burdening of any sort does not make for peace. Even in regular times when no peril threatens, when no illness, death, or other calamity seems near, we charge after unsubstantial things which have, at most, unsubstantial pleasures to offer—excitements which never stop the underlying hunger. And how these excitements die away! We are left, in the failure of grasping, duped and frustrated because nothing stays put together long, because object and desire alike are fuming, escaping, disappearing before we can settle into the imagined long enjoyment.

The impermanence of the melting snow, the dripping icicles, and our own tumbling thoughts implies, when we are willing to look, universal disquiet, unsatisfactoriness, and imbalance. And if there is ever to be peace in our minds of any lasting sort we have no reason to think it will come about from patience alone. Though we stand and stare hopefully at the blue, ascetic sky, still hunger and cold eventually creep over us; the winter shadows stretch out; regrets and wants renew their clamor. Indeed, we feel them now—the problems coming back like a wind, the sharp fears and restlessness, the projects and inconclusive ambitions, the charms of pastimes glimmering once again. To be ruled by these is familiar, ordinary, perhaps endurable, but we cannot call it satisfactory.

All craving is struggling on a hill of sand, which produces more weariness and suffering, not an ascent to peace; but we persist in spite of experience, because unexplained impulse drives us and because we simply do not see what else to do. Though we might even concede that the world is impermanent and liable to suffering, we wish to believe that, amid the boiling and subsiding of all phenomena, we at least have an indubitable stability, that we possess a self or ego which is superior to the surrounding flux and which we must exert all our strength to mollify, protect, and entertain. In Buddhist teaching, however, this self is nothing but a baseless concept, a mere device of language. A human being, like other creatures, is actually a dynamic pattern of mental and physical events shifting through time, without any unchanging part. It follows, then, that the ignorant compulsion to serve an imagined self can only deepen delusion and worsen error.

Now our hands and feet are getting cold. We hear no music in the waterfall and find no more beauty in the fantastic ice. Down here deep in the hollow, we see the sun vanishing behind the highest fringe of woods, and with it our rare sense of freedom is vanishing too. There is change happening and we do not like it. Shivering a little, rubbing our fingers, we look around at the way we have come with a sudden pang. Oh, let us turn back to home and warmth. Philosophy cannot stand the snow! But having come so far, having once made it to this strange place, we hold on a minute, for the remembered, lovely smile on a statue yet haunts us. How could he, the Buddha, seeing impermanence and suffering and the emptiness of the idea of self, still smile? How could he walk, unhurried and fearless, through a hopeless world? But maybe the world is not hopeless. And maybe he had found the cure for these dire conditions that assail us.

With our old human frailty beating within us, we try to concentrate, not stirring from our vigil beside the pool. Indeed, if everything in the world is impermanent, inevitably subject to arising and passing away, then it is unsatisfactory, untrustworthy, and prone to suffering. And if within this storm of transient feelings there is really no unique self to be found—no comfortable core of our personality to rely upon—then all our vanity is futile, for how should we ever feed an empty concept full with empty pleasures? And if all the objects we might crave are ultimately mist and illusion then we can never be satisfied, no matter how fast we labor. But if, by whatever happy means, we should *cease* to crave, would not the whole series of habit and affliction be broken?

We can scarcely imagine the consequences of such a relinquishment, such a release, but theoretically we can see that our ceaseless wanting, our insistence that things be this way or that, must always lead to sorrow. Still, it seems we want by instinct. We are born craving—how can we stop? Surely we would erase from our hearts all craving, hatred, and fear if we could, but we have no notion of how to do that. We lack wisdom.

The water trickles and gurgles over ice and stone and ruffles the pool before us, preventing any clear reflection. We lack wisdom, but the Buddha did not. Craving born and loosed leads on wretchedly to suffering; but craving, we must understand, does not erupt out of nothing; it is not inevitable and all-powerful. The Buddha traced down the fiery string of its causes and found its source at last in ignorance. By ignorance craving is fed; by ignorance the multitudes of living beings lose their way and fall to error and grief. And have we not been long in that company? Peering at the world through the mist of ignorance, catching blurred reflections, we misperceive, misunderstand, and take the illusory for the true, the trivial for the worthy. Not knowing, not understanding, not comprehending things in their actual nature, we succumb to flavors, colors, and fragrances, and give rise to craving and aversion again and again. Not questioning appearances, we pursue appearances and are deceived.

Whatever strength we have, whatever intelligence or will or nerve, will surely fail to bring us contentment if it is misdirected. Spiritual ignorance, this lack of true knowledge about reality, skews our faculties and sets us reeling, out of kilter, into the dangers of wrong perception. Taking the phantoms of the senses as real and true, trusting to baseless premises, assuming the unconfirmed, we reason, scheme, and strive, but never break finally free from suffering.

But if all craving could be abolished then our suffering would end. This thought, this memory of a teaching, stands out clear enough now against the pool, against the wasting snow, against the silent, uncomforting forest and the immeasurable heavens. Might it not also be true that our craving depends on the perpetuation of ignorance? Then our task must be to learn, to take such steps as will break down the wall of ignorance and let light fall into our confusion. If we could so train our minds as to look upon things without bias, then would not ignorance collapse and would we not escape the fatal sequence of wrong assumptions and wrong actions? Now, as anxious, guessing beings, we frown and tremble; but the Buddha's smile was unforced, because that imprisoning ignorance was all gone from him. Seeing things rightly as impermanent, unsatisfactory, and empty of self, he was not bound to run and grasp at anything, and his step was graceful and sure across the troubled earth.

The wisdom that shatters craving and releases the mind from suffering is not some esoteric, fortuitous inspiration but the gradual, built-up, practical understanding of the experience that flies through the senses. Liberation is obtainable—so taught the Buddha. There is a means, a path available to all who will exert themselves properly. We have heard of such a thing, have heard that it lasted down through the riotous, forgetful centuries and survives even now, powerful and free.

Abruptly we look up, as if we might see that path suddenly and literally ahead of us among the trees—a smooth, unambiguous road to safety. But as before, there is only the dormant forest with loops of vines and the clutter of dead wood and the thin, slow-melting snow. The waterfall of white marble looms above us, and above that the rocky hill with patches of sunlight. We are alone, just as before. Or perhaps—not quite as before. For now with a rare diligence deliberately kindled against the cold, with a mind keen on the living moment, we find the barest smile at last bending our lips. Now, how might this be? we ask ourselves. Oh, small presumptuous creature, shall *you* take your little steps, shall *you* escape the labyrinth of time?

Well, we wonder, what about it? Alone in the maelstrom of centuries, shall we yet make an unpredictable move? Water at our feet is gleaming as it runs off through the still, snowy landscape—and with it somehow our indecision has departed. Thoughtful, faintly smiling, we turn now and step judiciously down the course of the rivulet. What a wonder that we restrained ourselves this long—and all to win this small smile! So will is not dead in us yet.

Down at the creek bank again, we turn upstream along the way we came, walking as steadily as we can, bowing and bending again through the underbrush. It is still quiet but for a small bird or two chirping brightly somewhere. It is cold in the shadows, and we are negligible creatures, but shall we not keep going by such light as we have? We plod through slush and mud a long way back toward the upper end of the hollow and then begin to climb slowly and indirectly through the hardwoods and the green pines, following eroded, rocky lines in the hills. There is no hurry, only a mild persistence. The lunch we ate hours ago is all burned up, spent to the last crumb in woodsy explorations, and warmth is draining out of this bumbling frame, but what does that matter? We are getting tired, and that is to be expected.

And now this fair feeling, this hope, has come again, much as when we descended into the hollow, but this time not born of a full stomach or a sunny prospect but of—what shall we say?—attention and thought and effort? May it be so. Then, with such good help as still survives in the world, we ought to be able to strike some chips from the wall of ignorance.

Up on the high ground again, with the strain telling in back and legs, we emerge with a sigh from the woods to enormous cornfields and pastures spreading away under an enormous sky. Here the sun we thought lost still blazes, settling toward the horizon, yellow and dazzling over miles of snow. Far across the rolling land we see fences, trees, roads, electric towers, barns, and houses in an almost legendary vastness. In these dimensions we make our life. Here we exist for a little time—must we dream on into oblivion? We see distances to cross, and we have lost our former track in the snow; and around us, as before, the seasons display their epic mysteries. But by reflection, by attention, by disciplined action, we hope to turn ourselves toward certainty. Is it there, beyond that pond, across that wandering river, along that highway curving far away? A remembered smile is echoing now in us—this will make a beginning. Now to choose our way. Now to take another breath and go on.

2
READY TO LISTEN

When the world's harshness and the world's beauty drive us to serious reflection, when our pride is sufficiently undercut by sharp circumstance, we may at last begin to approach religion with a quiet step and a receptive mind. When we can quell the din of vanity, even briefly, we may begin to hear in more than a superficial sense and take in worthy ideas on how to live. With Buddhism a calm attitude is necessary, for this great system of truths is something to be comprehended rationally, explored, and proved against experience. Faith in these truths—if there is to be solid faith—depends on the individual seeker's gradual recognition of their value, not on any desperate enthusiasm or passion.

The Buddha was a man who claimed to have found the way to liberation from suffering and who taught this way to the world as a doctrine which is open to those who are willing to exert themselves properly. This doctrine is called in Pali the *Dhamma*, which means true nature, the essential law of existence, and the method of practice which leads to the overcoming of all suffering. The Dhamma is not the creation of the Buddha; he did not compose it, invent it, or design it. Rather he rediscovered it after an ardent, single-minded quest that culminated in his own complete enlightenment.

Far back in the inconceivable immensity of past time there have arisen, at remote, bright intervals, previous Buddhas; and sometime in the future there will be others yet, when all knowledge of the Dhamma has been long lost again. The Buddha of our present age, Siddhattha Gotama, rediscovered the way to deliverance, made it known, and spent his life teaching so that knowledge of the Dhamma might survive long in the world for the blessing of living beings. Having made his great search, having struggled in solitude until all hindrances fell away and the truth became clear, he spoke of himself as a *Tathāgata*—literally "one gone thus," meaning gone by means of the Dhamma to liberation, attained to the highest, gone to a state of absolute wisdom and peace. He had reached supreme knowledge and was free forever from the repeated afflictions of birth, aging, sorrow, and death. With his own work finished, he looked with compassion on the suffering multitudes of living beings and worked to point them in the direction of safety. The historical consequence of that work was peace and gladness for his followers and a continuing tradition of learning and practice.

According to Buddhism, the world with all its happiness and misery rises and falls, appears and vanishes, according to causes. All phenomena, from the trivial to the awesome, have necessary conditions and supporting factors; they do not just appear without reason, nor are they inexorably determined by fate. All phenomena, mental or material, arise out of impermanent conditions and become conditions themselves for the occurrence of further phenomena—on and on in *saṃsāra*, the cycle of birth and death. Any particular thing thus brought to being lasts only as long as the appropriate conditions remain intact. When the conditions disappear, the thing disappears. Existence, then, is a matter of cause and effect, of things being supported by other things—all of them liable to change and dissolution. Whether a certain event, welcome or unwelcome, will occur depends on the presence of the necessary conditions, the necessary causes, not merely on our wishes in the matter. Whether in the future we will become noble-minded or happy likewise depends on the presence of wholesome conditions and the absence of the unwholesome. If the right causes are in place, the effects will follow. The Buddha expressed this principle in a simple but profound formula:

> *When this exists, that comes to be; with the arising of this, that arises. When this does not exist, that does not come to be; with the cessation of this, that ceases.*

> (Majjhima Nikāya 115)

When the Buddha reached enlightenment he understood cause and effect; and what he taught others for the rest of his life was the cultivation of wholesome causes and the abandonment of unwholesome causes. It is not through any supernatural power of the Buddha that suffering is overcome, but through the intelligent, systematic action of the follower who carefully assembles the constituents of virtue and tends them until they ripen naturally. Faith, determination, and energy are necessary factors in this process, but they must be applied properly and in the right direction for happy results to occur. In the absence of understanding of cause and effect—of what leads to what—mere desire, longing, and enthusiasm are in vain. Therefore as a teacher the Buddha was concerned to impart knowledge, not just awe, devotion, and faith; for when a follower understands the mortal quandary rightly, and understands as well exactly what must be done to gain freedom, then he or she is at last in a position to advance spiritually.

We are speculating, struggling beings who wish for a happier, worthier life; and our chief problem in attaining it is not necessarily that we lack strength or intelligence or will, but that, stifled in the grip of ignorance, we simply do not see the world clearly; we do not know what should be cultivated and what should be avoided. Depending on faulty information about reality, we perform misguided actions of various sorts aimed at securing happiness, comfort, convenience, self-advancement, and so on; and since we understand clearly neither goal nor means we never get more than a shaky, temporary contentment. The solution to the problem is the cleansing of spiritual vision through self-discipline. When we become conscious of our poor perception and ill-founded reasoning and realize where the deficiencies lie, then, by following good advice, we can learn to stop doing those actions that produce the problem and to strive more systematically to distinguish the genuine from the illusory. As the actual features of the landscapes around us become clearer, so does the course we must follow to arrive at safety.

Such clear and useful perception, like other beneficial qualities, can be obtained and developed through proper exercise. If the right effort is made, blessings will naturally follow—cause and effect, once again.

The Buddha puts much emphasis on training the mind to see correctly, because as long as ignorance dominates the mind and falsifies our understanding, craving will continue to flame up and cause suffering. Under the oppression of ignorance we look confusedly upon the wealth and beauty of the world and think, "I want," unaware that all those goods are by their nature impossible to possess in the way we imagine—that is, as permanent, controllable, and exclusively pleasurable. We crave what we do not have—and immediately feel a lack. This lack is a kind of suffering. We reach and fail to get—this also is a kind of suffering. Or we succeed in taking hold of the desired object, and then, although we want to preserve it, it changes, fades, irrevocably dissolves—and our flimsy satisfaction gives way to further suffering. As long as ignorance spoils our perception we will continue to feel the urge to throw ourselves toward mirages, so if we ever hope to achieve independence of mind we must strive to expel ignorance.

The antidote to ignorance is wisdom *(paññā)*. Although we tend to regard wisdom as a fantastic form of mental perfection seldom or never found in the world, it is actually a quality which can occur in a great range of intensity, from the mildest light of understanding to the brilliance of a Buddha's insight. Moreover, wisdom, like all conditioned things, arises when the appropriate causes for it occur, which means that it is obtainable by one who seeks it in the right way, by providing those causes.

Buddhism recognizes three kinds of wisdom. First of all, there is wisdom to be had from thinking—one's own judicious examining, analyzing, and considering of experience. Then there is the wisdom gained through learning, through hearing and paying attention to an accomplished, skillful teacher. Finally, there is the wisdom that arises from mental development *(bhāvanā)*—the direct, intuitive understanding that results from disciplining the mind in meditation, or mindful, systematic contemplation of the functioning of nature. None of these three forms of wisdom, it is encouraging to note, is spontaneous or accidental; all are brought about by causes, by conscious actions which lie within the power of the individual.

Yet wisdom in itself, despite the grand connotations of the word, is not the goal of Buddhist practice. Wisdom is rather the supreme means by which one puts an end to spiritual ignorance, an end to craving, and hence an end to all suffering. We find in the Dhamma not the answers to all cosmological and metaphysical questions that might interest us, but rather those explanations that will be useful in eliminating suffering. Unmoved by blame or praise, the Buddha says, "Monks, both formerly and now what I teach is suffering and the cessation of suffering" (*Majjhima Nikāya* 22).

Because the world and all the phenomena within it are by nature impermanent *(anicca),* they are also unsatisfactory or suffering *(dukkha).* Whatever is impermanent, changeable, transitory, and prone to destruction is fundamentally unreliable and unsatisfactory and hence cannot be taken as a self, as a sustaining, lasting essence of our existence. Instead it should all be seen realistically as nonself *(anattā).* What we are is not, as we have assumed, a coherent self or ego inhabiting or owning a body, but rather a combination of five impermanent aggregates or groups of phenomena: material form, feeling, perception, mental formations, and consciousness. Our life is a dynamic, ever-changing pattern of these aggregates, like a stream which is called by a single name throughout its length yet changes constantly in width, depth, rate of flow, and quality of water as it goes along. With a self nowhere to be found other than as an abstract concept, no attempt to magnify a self can accomplish anything in the way of overcoming suffering. The Dhamma, being a practical doctrine, deals with realities, with the perceivable facts of everyday experience, in helping the practitioner to bring together the wholesome causes that naturally generate wholesome results. Well-being is the result of wise and virtuous action, and the Dhamma is a guide to such action.

Deep though the teaching of the Buddha is, its basic outline can be comprehended in simple terms. It is a religion that appeals to reason as well as faith, and reason is at once apparent in the central doctrine of the Four Noble Truths. There is first of all the overwhelming fact of suffering or unsatisfactoriness *(dukkha)* throughout all existence which again and again cuts short our joy. This suffering, like all other phenomena, comes about through causes; and the outstanding cause, the origin that the Buddha points to, is craving *(taṇhā)*—the ever-unsatisfied passion or desperate wanting for things that endlessly springs up in the heart and drives us here and there without understanding. Craving, moreover, produces rebirth, cranks the mortal machinery around and around, and forces the process of cause and effect onward, ever unfulfilled, from life to life, through higher or lower planes of existence, depending on the moral quality of our actions. It is not that there is some self or ego which continues in one form after another but rather that the stream of mental and physical events, of impersonal conditions, is constantly renewed by craving; and craving always gives rise to suffering.

But it is possible for suffering to be destroyed. It is destroyed when craving, its cause, is destroyed. The cessation of suffering, which is also the ultimate emancipation of the mind, is called *Nibbāna*. This is the supreme state, the removal of all greed, hatred, and delusion, the release from the repeated miseries of birth and death, the calming of all affliction. There is a way to this transcendent freedom; there is a pattern of mental and physical behavior which, if carried out properly, leads naturally to the ending of all suffering. This pattern, called the Noble Eightfold Path, consists of right view, right intention, right speech, right action, right livelihood, right effort, right mindfulness, and right concentration.

Such, in summary terms, are the Four Noble Truths—the truth of suffering, the truth of the origin of suffering, the truth of the cessation of suffering, and the truth of the way leading to the cessation of suffering. There is a phenomenon—a wretched and painful thing we call "suffering." It has a cause, namely craving. If that cause is removed, the phenomenon must disappear. That cause can in fact be removed and suffering can be eliminated through the practice of the Noble Eightfold Path. These are the profound matters that the Buddha understood and taught; these are what he thought worthy of attention, rational comprehension, and effort. The way we manage our lives—and the overall gladness or grief we experience—depends, whether we know it or not, on the degree of our understanding of these truths.

All of us acquire some kind of system of habit or belief ("philosophy" might or might not be too grand a name for it) according to which we act. It might be only the unarticulated conviction that we should do whatever gives us the greatest immediate pleasure; or it might be a thought-out devotion to an ideal of virtue or goodness. In any case, we become accustomed to acting in certain ways, and over time our moral character and our fortune are shaped by our actions. To the degree that we have been conforming to an ideal that is noble and true, we will gain benefit. To the degree that we have been conforming to what is base and false, we will experience suffering. It should behoove us, then, if we are still caught in doubt and suffering, to examine our habits closely and to explore reality, discover true principles, and revise our opinions and actions accordingly.

The Dhamma taught by the Buddha recommends itself to consideration by people who wish to explore reality, because it is "well proclaimed...visible here and now, immediately effective, inviting inspection, applicable, to be experienced by the wise for themselves" (*Majjhima Nikāya* 7). That is to say, the Dhamma is not obscure but clear, well set out, and logically arranged, so that an attentive person will find it accessible and comprehensible. It is visible directly in that the fundamental truths of the doctrine can be seen, noticed, observed by the individual practitioner: examples of what the Buddha talks about are available all around us in daily life. The Dhamma is also immediately effective because when it is practiced it brings gratifying results at once—for example, when someone consciously performs a kind deed and then observes in his own mind the immediate upsurge of joy. The Dhamma is inviting in that it is frank, plain, engaging, and open to study. Being inviting and full of valuable truths, it is applicable to present problems and leads onward gradually, according to the development of the student, to deeper understanding and eventually to full liberation. Moreover, the Dhamma is to be experienced personally, individually by the wise—not just appreciated theoretically, not distantly admired as the possession of another. The Dhamma is to be used for the specific good of each individual person.

Even if we received the Dhamma only as a compilation of bare doctrines alone it would be worthy of study, but in the Pali Canon we have as well a fascinating record of the life of the Buddha with many inspiring stories illustrating his character and method of teaching. When we hear some interesting teaching, particularly on serious matters of faith and religious practice, we naturally want to know something about the source of that teaching—what sort of authority it comes from, who he was, how he lived, what virtue or wisdom he exhibited, and so on. The Buddha, we find, practiced and taught a life of restraint, dignity, and compassion, never accumulating wealth or worldly power or seeking fame. Once he had reached supreme enlightenment he had, spiritually speaking, nothing further to do and might have retired to the forest permanently; but out of compassion for suffering beings he wandered about India for the rest of his life, selflessly teaching, advising, and encouraging others in the practice of the Dhamma.

> *There is one person whose arising in the world is for the happiness of many, for the welfare of many, who comes out of compassion for the world, for the profit, welfare, and happiness of human beings and deities. Who is that one person? It is a Tathāgata, an accomplished one, a fully enlightened one.*

> (Aṅguttara Nikāya 1:13, 1)

The Dhamma taught by the Buddha might have vanished in the following generations but for his establishment of a formal monastic order or *Sangha*, consisting of monks *(bhikkhus)* and later also of nuns *(bhikkhunīs)*. The Buddha entrusted the liberating doctrine in most detail to these disciples, who wished to live within an explicit framework of religious discipline and devote their lives to achieving liberation, but he also saw to it, through the regulations he instituted, that the Sangha would remain in close and beneficial contact with the rest of society. From those early days down to the present, the Sangha has given instruction and inspiration to lay people oppressed by the cares of the household life; and the lay people in turn have given the simple material supports that keep the Sangha alive. It is a noble and beneficial relationship, as the Buddha explains:

> *Bhikkhus, brahmins and householders are very helpful to you. They provide you with the requisites of robes, almsfood, lodgings, and medicine in time of sickness. And you, bhikkhus, are very helpful to brahmins and householders, as you teach them the Dhamma that is good at the outset, good in the middle, and good at the end, with its correct*

meaning and wording, and you proclaim the holy life in
its fulfillment and complete purity. Thus, bhikkhus, this
holy life is lived with mutual support for the purpose of
crossing the flood and making a complete end of suffering.

(Itivuttaka 107)

When the Dhamma is understood even slightly it leads the practitioner to a simpler, more graceful life, and when understood more deeply, when taken as one's central purpose, it leads on to a greater renunciation of worldly habits. When practitioners have gone so far as to devote their whole lives to the practice of the Dhamma they require very specific guidance. This is what the Buddha gave to the monks and nuns who followed him; and he gave, moreover, a formal system of monastic discipline, the *Vinaya*, which explicitly sets the bounds and details of proper conduct, regarding both morals and the practical requirements of celibate, communal life. It is this *Vinaya* which has protected and held together the Sangha for all these centuries and thereby ensured the survival of the Dhamma for the benefit of living beings.

Beyond the official, monastic Sangha, there is what is called the *noble* Sangha—the community of noble disciples who have reached or assured themselves of reaching full enlightenment. The practice of Dhamma is not only for the maintenance of a peaceful life right now but also and ultimately for the attainment of freedom from all birth and death; so the follower who strives rightly strives to become such a noble person, in whom the spiritual defilements are progressively reduced until they are eliminated entirely.

These three praiseworthy objects—the Buddha himself, the Dhamma, and the community of noble ones—deserve faith and reverence. When we revere what is worthy, when we rely on what is sound, we live deeper than the airy moment and we find strong ground to stand on.

But even if we can acknowledge, from a distance, the advantages of a reverent life, how are we actually to realize it in the face of our own apprehension? We might appreciate theoretically the nobility of Buddhist ideals yet still draw back, hesitant or frankly fearful, at the prospect of acting according to a system which might, for all we know, prove too hard for us. We harbor a nest of worries that spring up like wasps when we contemplate the challenges of an earnest religious life, and the stings discourage us. For one thing, we are perhaps a little reluctant to admit that we do need guidance, that our private speculations have, after long cultivation, borne no palatable fruit. Here a strange combination of embarrassment and pride may be at work—embarrassment at our inability to escape sorrow on our own (for we like to be thought capable and self-sufficient) and at the same time a tenacious pride in our intellectual independence, such that we really do not want to accept someone else's explanations of the universe. Furthermore, we might wonder, is not any application of faith and energy extremely unpredictable? Would it not be safer not to move at all, since moving might turn out to be a mistake? Then too, there is the worry that undertaking the Buddhist path with any seriousness might oblige us actually to change our opinions and our behavior in some respects and adhere to a standard that is not of our making. Do we really have the nerve or the humility for that?

What should especially encourage us and defend us from worries is the knowledge that Buddhism is a religion to be undertaken not through any extravagant hope but through rational faith founded on experience—that is, faith that grows together with understanding. An unthinking, purely emotional embrace of the Dhamma is insufficient; likewise a chilly, intellectual inspection of doctrine; but a moderate, sensible, open-minded investigation will produce plain and perceptible benefits that will stimulate further practice. When one listens, studies, and considers, and then finds the Dhamma inviting, one may think it worth testing. When one tests and finds the results encouraging, one gains a degree of confidence. With that confidence one then goes a little further, practices further, observing benefits as they appear. So, with progressive effort and reflection, one can follow the path in spite of worries.

Another encouraging sign is, paradoxically, the existence of the worries themselves; for why should there be such agitation, why should we flinch and second-guess ourselves so nervously in the midst of our casual society, except that we know intuitively that we are stuck in unsafe ignorance and must set out in some direction to find safety? We are hesitant, but we long for certainty; therefore it is reasonable at least to examine those aspects of the Buddha's teaching which catch our attention. Then one thing leads on to another; one noble utterance inspires deeper reflection; and after reflection the readiness to listen heightens; and by degrees the dimensions of the well-proclaimed Dhamma become manifest, and its beauty becomes more wonderful.

Always things in the world appear and disappear by way of causes—this is a vital principle to be kept in mind. With ignorance blurring the landscapes before us we will naturally fall to craving and aversion, and then our haphazard actions provoked by craving and aversion will produce haphazard results, leading to frustration and grief. But when we are ready to listen to the Buddha we will hear good counsel, and if we act upon it, making an effort in the direction of Dhamma, we can expect the growth of beneficial effects. Surely in our spiritual wandering we will make some mistakes, waste some time, and struggle through confusion, but as all that is merely the universal condition of unenlightened beings in any case, we ought not to be deterred from following the Noble Eightfold Path.

If the habits by which we have lived so far have not led us to any poise or wisdom we may rightly think it is time to apply ourselves with fresh will to those teachings that promise to satisfy both intellect and intuition. Faith should not be given lightly, nor withheld when a teaching proves worthy in experience. The Dhamma is inviting. It remains for now, thanks to the Buddha, available in the world for those who are willing to listen and to strive.

3
THE FLOWERING SEASON

Early on a spring morning after a night of thunderstorms we stand in the front hallway of our house and reach for the doorknob. Perhaps we have pondered our way into an especially philosophical mood today or perhaps the beautiful season has simply inspired us, but we haul the door open now with the unusual intention of making a pilgrimage into knowledge through this, the best weather we have seen for a long while. How many mornings have we trooped mechanically to work or set off around the block on a ritual stretching of muscles? But this shall be different—neither duty nor recreation. The morning is free, and instead of any dogged, salutary exercise we mean to take up the flowering season contemplatively, with mindfulness.

Silently the door swings past us, and to our joy spring blows in upon our senses with a moist breeze full of birdsong. Telling ourselves it will not last, telling ourselves to be alert, we go out, light-footed, down the sidewalk past wet lawns and blossoming trees and shrubbery. After all those months of stoicism, of holding our hopes together grimly, we step smiling through a world that for once does not threaten us but shines with indifferent beauty. We remember that clinging endangers our peace, and although we are not quite sure how far we should restrain ourselves, we at least manage to stroll at an easy pace and pass the cherry trees without a wistful backward glance. There will be more cherries, we expect, on the next block—or dogwoods or green cataracts of weeping willows or abundances of flowers all around. A few puddles of rain waver with the breeze, and the wet grass steams fragrantly under the sun, while we, as unnoticed visitors, float happily down the sidewalk through the neighborhood.

We have been, let us hope, sufficiently schooled by winter not to drop all mindfulness when delicate new life appears out of cold twigs, and not to forget the snowy lessons of impermanence. A month ago sleet was blowing across withered lawns; and in a few months these green, unrolling leaves of trees and bushes will be dry and falling; so this delightful season ought not to overwhelm us or make us forget the transience of all life. But there can be no fault, surely, just in knowing the beautiful to be beautiful, in seeing what answering gracefulness it arouses in us, in going about to perceive the noblest symbols in the season. We have not succeeded in reasoning our way neatly to liberation, and if the ebullience of spring can release our energy and restore our intuition we do well to take such pensive morning walks.

The lawns we pass are thick and disorderly, growing fast out of a complex of causes, with desired green blades and despised weeds flourishing together. Nature has no care for our tastes; left to itself it sprawls in heedless variety, distributing fruits and thorns as it will. But in our pleasant mood we admire both the weeds and the cultivated plants, for after the misery of winter all this thriving and flowering seems an encouragement to our besieged hearts. Most of our neighbors have spent time, last fall or earlier this spring, planting and tending trees, shrubs, and bulbs, and so we find, as we drift through the fair morning, more and richer colors than we might see in the uninhabited fields and woods. Here are cherry trees, then pear and redbud, along with plentiful tulips—so beautiful as almost to convince us that the world has at last revealed its lovely, secret nature.

On the corner of one lot we pause to admire a grove of old apple trees now coming into flower, but almost immediately we notice that the blossoms are not as abundant as we might expect from the size of the trees. Is it disease or something else that restrains them? Our gaze, which has been coasting along, now narrows down to seek the cause. The half-dozen decrepit trees have all been pruned much over the years, and now even many of the limbs that remain are obviously dead, with the bark corrupted and peeling. The general shape is preserved but the vitality is shrinking away. We consider the scene—the scarce apple blossoms on the slowly dying trees—and our mood of easy wonder begins to change.

One tree in particular draws our notice, for it is the smallest of the group, the most wretched and most severely cut. Once the trunk was triple, but over the years as deadness crept up much sawing was done, until now only one main limb remains—an absurd, out-of-balance, crooked thing whose branches themselves are mostly dead. At the top, a single living branch holds up a few white blossoms indistinguishable from the blossoms of the nearby trees. If we had not stopped, if we had strolled on with a casual look, we would have supposed the loveliness of this grove to be one whole, one categorical blessing for our minds; but now we must consider more critically, seeing the shifting balance of death and vigor so brilliantly illustrated before us.

The bark of the tree is an ugly, flaking ruin, dropping away from the dead wood. The stump-ends are slowly splitting up, fiber dividing from fiber with the same inexorable force with which they once clung together. Nature serenely and implacably goes about disassembling that which, in bygone springs, it constructed so marvelously. The final, ravaged limb cannot last much longer; there is no exception to the laws of change which revise all forms. Sloughs of bark and pieces of rotten branches lie about beneath the tree, and more will certainly fall until all that was the tree has resigned its pretenses and dissolved away. Yet this morning a faint thread of life still winds through the wreckage, making possible this sprinkling of flowers. Out of pink buds a few splendid white blossoms unconsciously open to the sun and add their beauty to the scraggly grove. Will there be fruit to follow in this last, declining season?

We have come at a rare, transitional moment, as the dwindling stream of vitality does what it can with failing substance. It is time to give up, we might think, but the tree does not. As the sun burns and the rain soaks the soil the impulse to flowering still breaks out, for the necessary conditions, although diminished, still hold together. Moths twitch and loop about the rotting trunk, while out of that one living, doomed branch the blossoms emerge—so few now but perfectly on time.

The misty air seems to be clearing up, so that the apple tree and all shapes stand out more sharply as we consider them. Here is more than an idle enchantment, more than a thoughtless, weightless lyric to enjoy and forget. Right before us the ancient urge toward life is overtaken by the principle of decay, and here (as everywhere, eventually) the pattern of flower, leaf, and fruit snags and unravels—prompting us now to stand back, widen our eyes, and ponder the awesome fact of impermanence which baffles all desire.

The cherry blossoms across the street are really not perfect, either; in fact they are nearly finished—already dropping into forgetfulness—but the eye is diverted from the truth by the swift opening of lush new leaves. Nature overlaps, so that, unless we watch with mindfulness, one novelty takes over for another and we never understand the elemental unrest beneath the moment. The forsythia bushes and the pear trees are half green now—their flowers do not last, either, nor do their leaves, nor any part of them. The spring we seize on dissolves into summer, and hope, ever deceived, is led around and around. Such is the grasping mind (itself forever changing) that the morning's prize will not serve in the evening, and the evening's dream must be replaced at every daybreak.

Here in this one pitiful apple tree we glimpse the gap in nature's show. Before its flowers are entirely gone and before the dead trunk is cut down and a healthy sapling planted in its place, we may contemplate the contradictions in living things and wonder what conclusions to make about our own life and the whole fantastic mass of perceptions we call the world. What do we feel about the slow death of the tree? We are not reconciled to this specific sadness; now we cannot easily turn our thoughts to apples and pears on the next block. If life as an abstract impulse flares up *elsewhere*, in other stems and petals, should we be mollified? We live here, in these dimensions of family, society, and landscape. Will one tree suit just as well as another, or one friend or one child? Where is the sense or meaning in all this flaring and subsiding?

Our pleasure at the apple blossoms' beauty is checked by the sight of their exhausted support—the expiring trunk we cannot keep out of our thought. And yet, at the same time, decrepitude is here transcended by beauty, as buds heroically expand once again. The contrast throbs with inescapable intensity—it is *dukkha*, unsatisfactoriness, suffering, the disquiet of compounded, changing things. Although we have come to think of *dukkha* as raw affliction only, it comprises also what is pleasing and graceful, for all that too is liable to change and disappearance and hence ultimately unsatisfactory. We wish to resolve the unease we see around us, to reach some happy certainty; but no meditation on flowers expunges the knowledge that they and the branch that bears them will soon disintegrate.

And at the same time, no resignation quite negates their brave splendor. Thus we hesitate, feeling the contradiction.

We can understand well enough that any form that occurs in this universe of cause and effect must come to an end when its causes disappear; but seldom do we see the rising and the falling so closely conjoined as here, where death and life pivot in a single branch. What can it actually mean for us who have trudged through winter and misfortune and need to restore ourselves with the perception of noble, inspiring things? Must we go on suffering? Must the thorns of disillusionment spread over all landscapes?

We look for certainties outside ourselves and find always incapacity and imperfection. Not to look, then, is the poor solution for many—to skitter past glaring facts, seek youthful orchards only, and wander on indefinitely, savoring chance beauty. But this will not do for anyone who realizes that the roaming appetite can never reach satisfaction among the impermanent fruits of the world and that no music on the senses can appease the cacophony of ignorance. If there is to be peace and certainty there must first be knowledge; and knowledge requires the exercise of our perception and judgment. This means, in the teaching of the Buddha, taking each phenomenon just as it is, just as it arises through our senses:

> *And how do those with vision see? Here a bhikkhu sees whatever has come to being as come to being. By seeing whatever has come to being as come to being he practices the way to dispassion for it, to the fading and ceasing of lust for it. That is how one with vision sees.*
>
> (Itivuttaka 49)

Spring has come to being; gardens and shrubbery have come to being; birds have come to being—and we should regard them simply as present facts brought about by causes, without assuming any eternal substance beneath them. All these things, having come to being, pass away, too; but we should not jump to the other extreme and make wrong assumptions of eternal annihilation, because, while formations vanish, they also continue to arise. What we observe are repeated facts and signs of the working of nature that we should use for mature reflection, not merely sensual enjoyment, so that we may regard them without delusion and passion and thereby free ourselves from the misery of clinging.

That we should seek dispassion amid the loveliness of the rain-freshened neighborhood seems strange—counter to the impetus of the season—until we remember that we have scarcely ever been free of passion and, not coincidentally, of trouble. Now that we think of it, passion always comes along on our walks, sits with us when we ponder, speaks when we speak. Passion, an officious companion, meddles in our perception, bends our judgment, and jostles us this way and that, keeping our view of reality unsettled. We *hope* we perceive shapes, sounds, tastes, and all accurately, but we suspect that passion gets into the process even before we notice it, introducing confusion and error. Rather than letting ourselves be upset by the impulse of the moment, we should observe phenomena simply, coolly, as they occur, as they arise or remain or pass away. If we do this we will perceive and judge more clearly.

The fact of impermanence, revealed both in fresh blossoms and in rotting bark, has halted our pleasant wandering, and we stand nervously considering whether we should determine to be glad or to grieve or to travel on in some kind of philosophical balance. Should we tear ourselves away from all reflection and loudly praise the glories of the season, insisting on the loveliness only? Or should we brood down to a tragic solemnity and declare the world a wasteland that deserves only tears? Or should we read the signs without trembling and try to desist from clinging altogether?

Perhaps we have already begun to read the signs. We have strolled down the fatal sidewalk and been captured by the apple grove, wherein birds sing and wet grass thrives and dying and living whirl together. Have we come to terms with nature yet? Shall we escape from here with any knowledge, with any beginnings of certainty? There is delight in this grove in the height of spring, and in the novelty of the whole burgeoning world, but let us rather take from here, if we can, not fruit or flowers but meaning, however uncomfortable it may be. Are we quite satisfied, reassured, by the knowledge that elsewhere young trees are growing healthily? In truth we are not. We perceive this present decay, we perceive *dukkha*, and we cannot, with any honesty, run off to obliterate the fact in a cloud of pleasure.

There is no pushing away of this knowledge once acquired. Let the spring sun glitter on all the grass blades, let the birds all trill together—still a somber truth has struck us like an arrow.

It is not, we realize, that we care so much for apple trees that do not belong to us, or that the permanence of this or that article of scenery is crucial for our well-being. Nor are we necessarily afraid to witness the natural dissolution of things. The meaning that assails us is both personal and universal. Never mind the scenery, never mind the incidental charms of the neighborhood—what about our own family, our children, our friends, and our own anxious, still uncertain life? What about all the mortal generations embroiled in birth and death? For we cannot miss the lesson in these dropping twigs and senseless blossoms—it is not these alone, but we too and all that is dear to us that shudder in the gales of impermanence. It may well be that today we expect untroubled work, friendly laughter, and comfortable rest; but what if these should be our final blossoms, our final branch of joys held aloft, while age or illness or harsh fortune at last arrives to torment us? How could we assume, against the testimony of apple trees, endless leisure in a tolerant season?

When we observe mindfully we see that things are imperfect *now;* so what will they be later on? A vision of earthly perfection tempts us: flowers and music and delicate breezes in unwithering gardens. But these gardens here, these lawns and groves, are as fair as any others and yet go bad, run to ruin, die off in parts despite the care of the gardeners. We too, as conditioned beings, grow for a few years and suffer afflictions; but as we can perceive and think, we must realize the futility of relying on imperfect nature to carry us to safety.

Yet must disillusionment always depress us? Might it not, like a great cleansing storm, wash the dead twigs from our path and purge the atmosphere of mist? By seeing things appear and disappear, by not clinging to any imagined permanence, we make it possible to travel to a real certainty. Earnestly considering the impermanence of all our joys and shallow consolations, we are led, in our own experience, to a recognition of the truth of *dukkha*—the worm in the bark, the choked-off sap, the inevitable withering of all worldly ventures. That vision, that storm wind, is cold enough, but paradoxically it opens up a wonderful landscape, with grand vistas and unsuspected hope. When we gaze upon the turmoil of existence and realize how we and unhappy multitudes chase pleasure and catch suffering, we are shocked into fresh investigation. Then the beauties of the natural world that before were objects of greed become objects of dispassionate meditation. Among other imperfect, ever-passing-away things, the curling apple blossom by its very impermanence turns our minds from sensuality and suggests the perfect—that which does not pass away.

We do not know what that is. The Buddha calls it *Nibbāna*. It is liberation, emancipation, the unconditioned, the unborn, the beyond. We wait, silent, straining, while the land still speaks in whispers that we cannot yet distinguish; but we have received a hint of a magnificence greater than the trivial delights we knew before. The wet, fragrant neighborhood that sparkles around us is only an assemblage of perceptions—a weightless fluff that the breeze will scatter. The destruction and decay here are real, indeed, but not permanent, either, not absolute. Always growing, withering, prospering, failing—such is the conditioned realm we grope through. It is certainly *dukkha*, unsatisfactory, but the very ambiguity, the dizzy contrast that we notice now, moves us out of complacency and into beautiful hope.

What we cannot get from any objective contemplation on nature is guidance on how to act so as to escape recurrent suffering. For that we must turn to the Buddha. The ambivalent, restless world reiterates to the careful listener the fact of suffering and the idea, the possibility, of liberation from it; but once we have set out on a serious search we need the Buddha's masterful advice on where and how to apply our strength, what we should look for, and what we should avoid. Perhaps we never would have pressed on even this far in reflection this morning had we not before learned something of the Dhamma, the great doctrine; but as it is, having begun to consider the relentless sequences of nature and the desperate reach and fall and reassertion of life, do we not sense the need for specific knowledge, for a remedy of wisdom?

The examples of lovely flowers and perishing wood, of blossoming and collapse, turn our minds forcefully to the processes of *saṃsāra*—the arising and the passing away—which, the more we reflect, seem to resolve into the single process of change, wherein no permanent peace is found. The fragmentary songs of birds, the enchantment of splashing streams, the brief richness of the redbud trees all show this quality of imperfection, of the inevitable trailing away of one thing into another. The single evaporating puddle and the whole season with its suns and forests repeat the same theme of temporariness and disquiet, and reveal the futility of looking in beautiful objects for spiritual purity.

Living now with a mind that questions, troubled by suffering, born to see beauty and the decay that follows it, how shall we resign ourselves to the continual destruction? Surely there is something better possible—so we guess from the uprushing spring season which, before it declines, carries us to this height of hope. If we pay attention to the teaching of the Buddha we may discover a solution which does not occur to instinctive nature. It is a kind of action which does not aim at what nature aims at— that is to say, virtuous, consistent, wise action.

That an ideal of virtue or purity should appeal to human beings is in itself a cause for cheer. It will not entertain us or fill our stomachs, but it at least begins to cure our loneliness and lack of purpose in the storms of heedless nature. The Buddha saw that only through virtue, concentration, and wisdom is there a way to transcend our otherwise lugubrious destiny; for these powers treat the unseen disease of craving, which otherwise festers on unhindered through all our efforts to sustain and amuse an imaginary self. To beings burning with craving and ignorant of any release, the anti-virtues of avarice, aggression, and opportunism might seem entirely natural (and so they are, in the grimmest sense) but in practice they give no peace and only string out misery endlessly. For those, however, who look deeper, who guess at freedom from all hunger, the idea of liberation begins to shine.

Against the universal rage of grasping the Buddha teaches relinquishment. Against the frenzy of vanity the Buddha teaches selflessness. The goods of the world, when lusted after, turn poisonous; and the ignorant urge to exalt ourselves sinks us into sorrow. We would have all the world belong to us, but after all scheming not a grass blade or a raindrop does. All things change, including this mind and body, and all drift out of our power. For freedom, then, for calm, for goodness, we must cease from craving and clinging. Even what we regard as most intrinsically ours— these very sense faculties and the perceptions that flicker through them— ought not to be so misunderstood but instead should be regarded realistically, without grasping. The trees with their white coverings of blossoms are not ours. The lawns, the shining puddles, the houses we pass are not ours. Mere light and color reach us; sound and smell roll in with nobody's name attached and roll away again.

Now we have lingered long enough at this spot, perhaps. We have not touched a flower, but we find that we carry away bouquets of wonder, whose scent is rarer than any earthly fragrance here. If an apple tree will blossom into its last season so bravely, how shall we, endowed with a human mind, spend our fine spring on folly?

Shall we move on now and send this body, while it yet obeys us, farther into the fields of reflection? The day is vast, with unknown limits. Down the long, flowering block, voices cry out cheerfully, a car or two glides by, the birds quarrel and sing, and the breeze, light and sweet, drifts over the neighborhood and wanders away.

4
REGARDING
WORLDLY FORTUNE

Returning home from work or from a morning of household errands, we pause on the front porch, holding bags and packages in one arm while trying to work the door key, so absorbed in daydreams that we hardly know what the body is doing—when we hear the telephone ringing within. At once our automatic motions are speeded up until, hopping and stumbling, we shove our way inside and drop our burdens on top of the table in the hall. There really is no time for reflection, but somehow in the agitated moment before we seize the telephone on the table we feel a worrisome sensation of coercion or dependence, as if we were not acting out of our own will at all but being pushed, being accelerated incomprehensibly through a series of habitual motions. Neither looking nor listening with any attentiveness, we have arrived home today just as a thousand times before, and now when the telephone signals us we are not to any degree awakened but only stung to a quicker obedience. The ringing occurs and we lurch to answer. Why?

Let us allow ourselves a beat to consider. There is need; there is desire. We pace through weary, routine days, and any tiny irregularity, any promise of newness, is enough to make us start up, for under the surface dullness there runs the fiery stream of dissatisfaction, endlessly twisting and searching. We are always wishing, we dimly realize, for things to be different, to be better, to be fresh and free. This day and every day we go out and come back again with the old disquiet, looking for some long desired message, for the urgent intelligence which will marvelously remake our lives and launch us into unguessable adventures. Blessings and opportunities might fall within our reach; answers to desperate inquiries might at last relieve our fears. Then too, we have not entirely shaken off apprehension of troubles—the application turned down, the rejected request, the rebuff to our hopes, the new danger to our security and comfort. Will the universe not stop its fitful harshness toward us? Will we not, at some definite culminating hour if not this one, find our deserved fulfillment?

The telephone shrills, and even as we take hold of it there runs through us this sense of the up-and-down, unappeased commotion of life, the surge and retreat of our longings, the inconclusiveness of our efforts, the happiness that laughs and disintegrates and will not stay. This telephone call, this communication about to happen, might be the beginning of certainty, of assurance, of fortune without pain; and although, realistically, we doubt it, we cannot quell the twinges of hope and fear. What if we should be surprised with joyful news—a fabulous gift, an unlooked-for promotion—or with shocks and disasters? In either case time rages on unchecked, and there will be no conclusion to our wandering. Across the imagined future we see no place where change may not overtake us, where agitation must of necessity cease. We have, indeed, no justification for supposing that the world must ever conform to our preferences, however much we wish it would.

We have the telephone in our hands; we lift it eagerly. A voice comes through—and then we relax into another mode of habit. The telephone call is ordinary, and we summon up a sprightly tone, the one we all use to assure each other that we are cheerful and competent managers of our lives. "Ah, yes, just fine! It sounds wonderful. I look forward to it. Thanks. Fine, see you then!" And now with the telephone down again, we look around, a little vaguely, for some new idea or promise from fate, as we feel hope and apprehension still alternating slowly within us.

Outside this unquiet mind, and apart from our subjective notions, is this world really a paradise or a wreck? To properly evaluate any object, from a mosquito perched on our wrist to a whole flowering landscape, we surely need both descriptive facts and the skill to read through them to principle. We could sit down and tabulate abundant horrors of this human realm, certainly, and abundant beauties as well; but we do not know how far our personal view distorts our computation, and we do not even know whether anything really is to be gained by pronouncing the world lovely or hideous. Let us pause, then, and consider how the Buddha describes this ambivalent world.

In the largest terms he sees it, as we already know, as *dukkha,* unsatisfactory, fundamentally untrustworthy. But this world is not therefore to be spurned as meaningless, for within it there can be found the means to liberation: the revealed Dhamma and the innumerable signs and evidences which we might use to awaken our understanding of this Dhamma. What makes the world so maddeningly hard to measure is the prevalence here of eight "worldly phenomena" *(lokadhammas):* gain and loss, fame and lack of fame, praise and blame, pleasure and pain. These volatile phenomena upset our predictions and our longing for stability, bringing now happiness, now affliction, oblivious to our welfare; and amid their uproar we labor on wretchedly, trying to separate the desired from the undesired.

Why, we might inquire, should we not have gain without loss, satisfying fame, timely praise, and unbroken pleasure? This is the way the world *should* be, should it not? We rebel against an empty, unexplanatory sky, sharpen our craft, scheme for a fantastic fortune—while triumphs and calamities succeed one another, applause and jeers are heard, some speculators gain and some lose, and for all our urgency no satisfactory end to anxious uncertainty appears. But are there not, we plaintively ask, some few who are especially favored—those sages free from bad luck and failure—and should we not be able, somehow, to share their luck?

We would have security and ease; but before we can claim them we must have knowledge. Now let us look. Where exactly are the lucky enjoyers of one-sided fortune? Let us reflect over space and history until we can realize that, in fact, there are none at all. Sages too endure the same mundane circumstances as we—they fall sick, suffer injuries, meet with unwelcome changes—but their wisdom sees past the incidental to the universal, to the certainty of change that is best coped with by equanimity. Wisdom does not alter the world; it lets the sage transcend the world. Anxious pain strikes only those who cannot understand the impermanence of all these desired and feared states and who cannot extricate themselves from the profitless flux of desire and aversion. Real independence is the result of reflection and disciplined, honorable behavior.

What are these gains and losses that so engross us? They are matters of possessions and perquisites—at bottom just temporary worldly conventions. When we acquire some valuable material object, for example, we cling to it; we presume to own it—insofar as a compounded, perishable thing may be owned. This is gratifying, perhaps, while the object stays put in our living room or in front of our house, but since all phenomena have the nature to dissolve—and since we ourselves are impermanent and mortal—the gratification, like the object, should rightly be seen with insight as a passing thing that we should not allow to ruffle us. Gains of money, food, lodging, clothes, and the other forms of wealth certainly have their concrete advantages, their conventional, temporal uses; but we should note that the concept of gain is necessarily bound to that of loss, of decrease and disappearance; so the best choice in the face of both is equanimity. If today we lose some item we value, we might well reflect that such a separation was certain to happen sometime. If today gain comes to us, that is fine, but we ought not assume that nature has decided to accommodate us forever.

Unfortunately, the tendency of the ordinary mind is to expect gain as the natural result of living, and to imagine that increase is normal and that decrease or loss is the sign of a life gone calamitously awry. If our possessions and powers do not expand, or if they fall away, we take it badly and become unduly upset, grieving over the injustice of fate. Perhaps we even suppose that it is the function of a properly running universe to supply us with more and better things; so loss does not appear natural to us at all but shocking, frightening, and intolerable.

Such a view is not based on any realistic assessment of experience. The world is endlessly variable, full of annoyances and perils, and all living beings partake of its uncertainties. Both the wise and the foolish meet with gain and loss, there being no neat and satisfying apportionment of prizes; but the foolish in their delusion suffer more, supposing that gain must grow and swell and never cease. Where the idea, the obsession, of gain is weaker the suffering attendant on loss is weaker as well; and one who less and less occupies himself with such accumulations can gather instead a wealth of wisdom.

Besides the getting and losing of things conventionally thought valuable, we must deal with the interchange, interplay, and instability of fame and lack of fame, or repute and disrepute. We desire, with pitiable doggedness, to be recognized, respected, deferred to; but from what deep unease does this desire proceed? Do we not have some secret doubt about the reality or quality of our "self," such that we yearn for assurance in the eyes of others? Ah, if *they* admire us perhaps we are safe! But such evidences of honor as the world gives out are, like the coarser gains and riches, inevitably unstable—sometimes seemingly merited and sometimes not, but never making a durable defense against *dukkha*. If we allow ourselves to be flattered by recognition we grieve all the more when recognition is withdrawn. Oh, once we were known! Once we were honored, and faces turned eagerly to smile at us! Once the murmur of welcome surrounded us! To be alone, to be neglected, causes pain to the extent that we expect company and attention.

On the other hand, when there is no expectation of being considered important, there will be no suffering as a consequence, whether or not fame comes or goes. If we stroll out in the impartial summer sunshine and no one knows us, should our contentment be impaired? The sky does not know us and the earth does not notice our passage, true. Do the morning-glories then bloom any less colorfully? In all seasons of fortune the seasons of nature revolve impartially before the watchful mind.

When fame or repute is desired but not achieved it causes pain. When it is achieved it fluctuates, and causes pain. Insofar as it exists at all, it is a transient notion in others' minds. Why should we be so concerned over that which, if it comes, will certainly depart, leaving others indifferent and ourselves regretful? To hanker for fame, or to lament the fame lost, is to resign a part of our welfare to the control and negligence of others, so that we become less, not more, secure.

Even if we withstand the allure of fame we are still apt to succumb to anxiety over two other worldly phenomena—the everyday praise and blame we receive. We perceive these as separate, independent things, as creatures of utterly distinct species—one lovely and one loathsome—and we see no reason why we should not (by prudent selection of friends or our own manifest merit) obtain plentiful praise and escape all blame. But despite our theories and our wishes, whatever compliments we get seem, in the event, to fall somewhat short of the level we would like, and moreover are too often overwhelmed by the stings (mostly unjust, we think) of criticism.

While virtuous behavior is assuredly more likely to elicit praise than blame, worldly uncertainty and the whims of human beings make any praise a tenuous, arbitrary thing outside our control, which a sensible person should regard skeptically, knowing it as impermanent noise without nourishment. If we have done good work, if we have made some estimable achievement, should that not suffice for our satisfaction? If it does not, and if we are ever hungering for somebody to *say* how splendid we are, surely we have not yet arrived at full maturity. We can hardly achieve independence from the vicissitudes of worldly life by courting more uncertainty in the form of others' haphazard favor. Praise, moreover, even of extraordinary frequency and richness, simply cannot drown out the blame which periodically comes our way. Praise may even make blame harder to bear, because unless we are very attentive we may become so attached to a fantastic, false view of reality that any slight or criticism or neglect seems an outrage.

Praise and blame are just two natural phenomena that happen to mortals. We may definitely attract one or the other through our conscious behavior, through the momentum of our entire character, but there is still no way to get only praise, as both phenomena depend on the infinitely varied, capricious notions of others. Virtue, on the other hand, arises from our own work, wrought by our own faithful effort. In Buddhism we are advised to cultivate virtue not because virtue guarantees the annihilation of blame and the magnification of praise, but because virtue is a blessing in itself, requiring no outside recognition, that soothes the heart and lifts it above the storms of fortune.

The last two of these worldly phenomena are pleasure and pain. These are simply the mundane shocks of fate, the back-and-forth ill luck, good luck, sickness, health, ease, and affliction. They come and go in the lives of all; but the particular events are less important to our well-being than the degree to which we react to them with greed or aversion. One person might be burdened with many misfortunes yet live serenely while another, though apparently enjoying prosperity and pleasure, might seethe over his failure to get all he actually wants. For this world remains, despite its beauty, part of *saṃsāra*, the cycle of birth and death, wherein craving necessarily leads to grief. If we suppose that happiness requires an unending fountain of good fortune we will never have genuine happiness, because the world does not function that way; rather, genuine happiness comes from a wise adaptation to natural circumstances.

This adaptation is not a mere cleverness in arranging one's worldly business for maximum personal advantage, but rather a noble attitude toward the impermanent universe. If one can so restrain oneself as not to think of gain, fame, praise, or pleasure as personal properties or indeed as essentials for contentment, then no misery can follow from their natural disappearance. The Buddha says that when an ordinary, unlearned person experiences any one of these worldly phenomena he does not regard it properly: he does not reflect that this gain or loss is impermanent, ultimately unsatisfactory, and liable to change; he does not understand it rightly. Then that gain or loss or other potent state overwhelms and dominates his mind. He cherishes the gain and abhors the loss, and being involved in "favoring and opposing" he cannot get free from suffering. The learned, noble follower, by contrast, reflects well on the arisen phenomenon and, knowing it as it is, does not allow his mind to be overcome by it. Unimpeded by favoring and opposing, he is able to free himself from suffering.

It is not that the sagacious person escapes all misfortune in this life (for no one does that) or that he simply endures misfortune nobly (which he does), but rather that he does not allow either agreeable or disagreeable experiences to upset his balance. He regards gain, fame, praise, and pleasure just as calmly as their opposites, remembering their untrustworthy nature.

Such equanimity or detachment contrasts with worldliness—the fascination with trivial, mundane things, the appetite for the superficial. Certainly most of us are of necessity much involved with the material requirements of jobs and family duties, but this does not mean we must become cynical, worldly, and heedless of the religious requirements of our hearts. We need not be perfect to revere what is perfect and to emulate it as well as we can. The goodness, equanimity, and honor we sometimes see in exceptional persons do not prevent them from doing their work and coping with life's troubles; rather these qualities guide and discipline their practical abilities.

When we are not unduly absorbed in trivial wishes—not narrowly yearning for luck and worldly sharpness—we can consider more attentively matters of real need and value, namely the cultivation of virtue, concentration, and wisdom. These qualities will console and refresh the mind over years and lifetimes, while momentary excitements expire emptily in the moment, leaving behind the same sad hunger for pleasure and novelty.

In the hallways of our houses and in the mazes of our uncertainty we call out for news, hoping for the good or the extraordinarily favorable only, though gain and loss, fame and lack of fame, praise and blame, and pleasure and pain are always storming across the landscape of *saṃsāra*. The sage, however, aware of their variable nature, does not look to these phenomena for his peace, but simply lets them pass, contemplating their impermanence.

The practice of Dhamma does not reverse the course of nature but gives the practitioner the means to live peacefully according to nature. The greatest obstacles to be overcome exist in our own minds in the form of greed, hatred, and delusion; and we cannot attain true peace as long as these defilements remain in place, no matter how temporarily lucky or unlucky we might be with respect to these eight worldly phenomena. To the degree that we manage to maintain equanimity toward them we will be free of the rage and despair they otherwise create. This equanimity, happily for us, is not some superhuman stoicism that we are expected to forge out of nothing, not a blank numbness or callousness, but rather a mature sense of balance and nonexcitement that comes about naturally through seeing things clearly. When things are seen clearly—as impermanent, unsatisfactory, and empty of ego—then there is no gale of partiality to upset the mind.

Here in the hallway, where we have often paced in worry, there are doorbells and telephones to answer. Here the news goes back and forth; astonishment, complaints, and laughter ring out and fade again; life changes and we must stay vigilant to bear the changes with dignity. The Buddha says, "The eight worldly phenomena keep the world turning and the world keeps the eight worldly phenomena turning" (*Aṅguttara Nikāya* 8:6). This world is just *saṃsāra*, the running on, wandering on, piling up of temporary factors; and when distracted living beings struggle without wisdom they only add to the universal commotion. Independence from this *saṃsāra* can only come about when, by rightly seeing and rightly acting, one steps back and abandons craving for that which has no true substance.

Standing quietly in the hallway, we begin to notice our own breathing going on steadily beneath the dance of thought. We see photographs on the wall, notes, and mementos—all these opportunities for reflection, each with its particular significance and, besides that, its temporary, factual presence. We drag our fingers over the shiny, dented wood of the table, pondering the bare sense of touch. Then there is the smell, faint and sweet, of flowers in a vase. We hear cars passing on the street. Gazing around, we see books, magazines, rugs, furniture—just shapes and colors in complicated arrangements. Dust glimmers before us in the air, silently turned and tumbled by the motion of our feet or our breath. The world here and all about is built of causes, spun and rocked by causes; and we as sentient beings must everywhere sense the endless upsurging of contrasts. There is no real safety in familiar, comfortable places, even in this one, because luck and loss blow in and out of all rooms.

These eight phenomena are just the background against which we living beings act; and it is action—our own intended action, not another's—which constructs our character and leads us to safety or danger. If we cling to gain, fame, praise, and pleasure, and fail to contemplate their temporary nature, we renew suffering and never achieve more than incidental, inconsistent happiness; but if we contemplate calmly, not clinging, and set about doing those beneficial things within our power, we advance ourselves toward the ultimate safety and happiness.

Now with a new deliberation we observe our keys lying on the table alongside our packages and miscellaneous stuff. Every day we act, we carry out purposes, churning through our business with so little poise. What if toward all these changing things we were to establish mindfulness, so that contemplation might become not a rare and tedious exercise but the free function of a balanced mind? Just to be aware of these states as they come and go is a worthy start—to know them as not ours and not subject to our will. Thus much futile grieving would be prevented, and we might earn more of real serenity. When the mind is not distracted by the imaginary and the unsubstantial, it can better take care of important matters here and now.

The Buddha has summarized what should be done as "to abstain from all evil, to cultivate the good, and to purify one's mind"—three forms of intentional action that bring benefit regardless of mundane gain and loss, fame and lack of fame, praise and blame, pleasure and pain. We should try, by restraining our hungry senses and adhering to noble standards, to keep all unwholesomeness from infecting our views and behavior. We should try to arouse and develop good mental states—not merely waiting for a mood of kindness to sprout like a chance flower among weeds. We should try, further, by observing, meditating, and contemplating, to distinguish and then remove all roots of defilement within our minds. This is the work of Dhamma, the work that leads, past all the mishaps and excitements of luck, to emancipation.

With a smooth breath now we stretch out our hands to straighten our pile of packages. With just such careful gestures we settle our minds in the midst of worldly disturbance. Here are books to read. Here are purchases to maintain the household. Here are lists of chores that we are capable of doing. Now then, shall we not go about our business with a calm purpose? A light from the windows shines across the floorboards of the hall. It is not much; it is not splendid; but it makes our present steps clear enough. So we go on through the moment to straighten things as we can. The day will run on with its adventures. Voices will reach us, changes will come, but before us, in the stillness, the path leads on.

5
NOT GOOD
BUT BEAUTIFUL

I t happens sometimes that, without intending it, we wander past fun to philosophy and wonder. We go out blithe and eager, ready to enjoy a manageable pleasure, but suddenly or slowly the excursion changes; the gravity of what we see exhausts our smiles; the easy trail is lost; the land darkens; and ancient skies gleam down on us. What we thought, what we assumed, what we trusted in seems a frail conceit, with awesome immensities looming all around us. We meant, on the whole, to have a good time (and would that not make a terrible epitaph?), but time will not be held; and we lose our place and wander abashed and breathless, deep in ignorance. Do we then try to learn? Or do we cringe from knowledge? Each wanderer secretly decides and lives on with the consequences.

There are many ways into the unknown but it might be like this. We go out to hike in a park, persuaded by the lovely summer weather and the allure of remoteness. It is not exercise, exactly, that we seek, but perhaps some restoration of aliveness, some freshened and intensified perception, some mildly atavistic joy of tramping through natural scenery far away from the sounds and sights that annoy us. We are looking forward to a stimulating, entertaining change from our routine, hoping that a couple of hours among pine trees and boulders will allow us to stop thinking so much about our problems and to absorb the beneficence of nature.

On the epic morning we abandon the city and the suburbs and plunge into the countryside. How huge the land is, now that we see it again. What promise! What possibility! With a spirit of romance rising, we are keen for new vistas and the glorious scent of forests. We wish to climb a mountain by an original path or to circle a lake beautified with brilliant wildfowl or to stroll through soft meadows full of flowers and butterflies. We imagine we shall soon be reclining on some fair height with vines and waterfalls and idyllic forest below us falling away into the mellow distance. Just the antidote for the discontent that plagues us! With all our worldly skepticism, we have kept a yearning, indefinite faith in the goodness of country untouched by human beings—and we mean to revel in that goodness if we can, to cleanse ourselves of gloom, and to reassure ourselves of a radiant and wonderful universe.

Some while later when we reach the park the sun is standing high and the big, blank land lies silent before us. At last no roads, no cars, no glare and screech of traffic—just as we wished. But we delay a moment, oddly conscious of being dropped down with a crash into this strange, silent moment. The shopping centers and roaring highways have vanished, and now, it seems, we must *enjoy*. How should we go about it? We are getting ready to take off into an approximation of wilderness, looking down a damp trail full of undistinguished rocks; and although there are green slopes of forest around us, we are a little chagrined that we do not find it all instantly marvelous. It is pretty, certainly scenic, but it still seems disturbingly factual and ordinary—with natural elements arranged in such-and-such a way, with tree trunks, weeds, mud, and flies. This is a little disappointing. The bark we brush with our fingers has a prosaic roughness; the sun here is as hot as in the city; and the rocks underfoot are no more beautiful than those anywhere else. We close our eyes and feel our breath going in and out in familiar rhythm. Here we are again, just as before, not yet outside the ordinary. We open our eyes and shake ourselves briskly. Well, then! We shall just have to find a way to get into sympathy with the character of this place. It was rash to suppose we had only to dash out of our house and trot over a hill to get inspired. We came for a hike, so let us be going.

We start down the trail through mixed sunlight and shadows at what we hope is a nice contemplative pace. In the low places there is sticky mud, it having obviously rained hard recently, but mostly the path is firm enough and not too steep, curving through sweet-smelling green woods. A breeze shuffles in the leaves above, and white fluffs of seeds float all around. Intricate and pleasing sights entertain us—passageways in the undergrowth and stony prospects that flash through the mind and begin to give us some sense of the multiplicity and abundance of the natural world.

So on we go, away from civilization, as we like to think, smiling earnestly at the hills, trying hard to be at ease. Certainly we are glad to have begun this escapade, but still we feel somewhat awkward and estranged from the apparent cooperation of oaks and earth and sky. The mute, objective world does not at once adopt us. The sun, the breeze, and the slowly steaming ground seem to have their own communion, apart from us who are looking eagerly this way and that for the barest welcome or acknowledgement.

In spite of our resolve to let our city-heated thoughts cool down, we find, in the monotony of our hiking, some not entirely agreeable reflections occurring. Are we presumptuous outsiders here, incapable of fitting in? Have we stood too long on carpets to be comfortable on gravel and pine needles? Must we trudge through the backwoods and sleep on rocks for years before we become worthy to delight in nature? Or—more gloomily—have we wrongly inferred serenity behind a charming appearance? How much does our desperate wishing skew the patterns that our senses show us? Through our frantic days and calculating nights we have retained the treasured conviction that there are places, particularly these surviving regions of wilderness, which are good in themselves or especially rich with some essential splendor of existence. So why, when we come out here, sincere and receptive, do we still feel such distance and indifference in nature? Why do the beautiful, mysterious hills at last seen close remain in a profounder sense as secret and remote as ever?

It is not easy to turn off thought, to abandon worry in favor of a joyful basking. The odor of wildflowers and the chirping of birds, to whose enchantment we would give ourselves up, do not lull us at all today but simply produce more puzzling sensations. We are troubled by the ambiguity of our desire: do we wish, at bottom, just to doze and bask, or to see through all confusion in a brilliant revelation? And regardless of our desire, what is actually possible within the limitations of this mortal world?

While we might have preferred a thoughtless enjoyment in our hike, it is at least encouraging that here we can formulate questions more clearly than amid the busyness of work and home. After so many years of hurrying through crowded buildings, we find ourselves curiously isolated and uncertain even in a few acres of forest—here where we were hoping to find relief and satisfaction immediately. Now no voices break in on our thoughts; no duties blunt the sharpness of the moment; no tedious dreams take hold of us; but we tramp on noisily without inspiration. We do not fit easily into this ancient, earthy world. Perhaps we may yet, but right now we keep an eye out for thorns and worry about losing the tenuous trail. The inner goodness of the landscape, long our romantic ideal, has yet to appear; and we hike along moodily with our solitude heavy and unrewarded.

After a while, when much scenery has flowed through our senses, we begin to wonder whether the lack of spontaneous joy is our own fault, whether a more determined pursuit of beauty is not called for. So we step along for a minute with a quick and narrow glance, trying to catch the rare sight, the exceptional color in the breeze-ruffled leaves, the secret darting of birds through thickets. But this gets tiring fast; it seems too clumsy; and, as we are pouncing on potential delights, we must wonder how it differs from ordinary greed. For surely we are aware of our habitual longing for pleasures of the senses. Is greed for natural scenery so much superior to the other sorts?

The trail now descends into a valley, and soon we are walking beside a swift, wide creek full of boulders. Trees stretch out over it, dropping indistinct shadows. The water is still high from the last rain, here foaming white as it gushes between boulders, and here gliding and spreading in great green surfaces—water taking on color and giving it up with effortless magic. We begin to relax a little as we watch, as if the sight of all that external motion allows us to turn away from our own mental flood. Before us there is a great mixing of currents, an exhilarating sweep and melting of curve into curve, a pouring of coolness beneath the hot sun.

Here a fragrant mist seems to surround us, and a wet, rushing sound covers our footsteps as we clamber down through weeds and mud to get near the water. It is the magnetism of wild vigor, perhaps, that draws us—the inexplicable attraction of natural power concentrated here; and we begin to feel cheered and stimulated. A stretch of boulders, both submerged and dry, confronts us, and we pause for a moment pleasantly considering the manifoldness of the scene. We have no need to hurry, so we are content to climb on these near slabs and projections—just fooling around as a child might in the summery complexity of water and warm stones and piled-up driftwood. At length we manage to climb onto a flat slab surrounded by a fast current. Shall we take a rest? Here we can sit down in a convenient blotch of shade—an admirable island for meditation, just the thing we needed. True, the stone is a bit less comfortable than we would have wished, but we are glad of even this small accommodation for us in the impersonality of nature.

Resting here beneath a long, drooping branch, smelling the sweetness of the wet summer, admiring the sunny scenery, we are quite ready to drift into a reverie, except that certain ideas continue to intrude on our peace. The beautiful swirling of water around this rock, we observe, is a result of a recent rain—there is a cause behind the phenomenon; and as causes are impermanent we know we cannot expect an eternal supply of pleasing patterns. The water level rises and falls, bringing motion and noise, mud and driftwood, irrespective of our pleasure or the requirements of fish. We are lucky, then, to have arrived at this moment when the creek is fresh and full and mixes so prettily in white and green and amber; but in relaxing into the pleasure are we not abandoning something of our independence and balance and giving way to incautious partiality? For when one fortuitous moment is seized upon, another, by implication, is not—is feared or despised—and since we do not control the changing character of nature our delight must remain, as it was before, pale and brief and incapable of preserving us from suffering.

We sigh, shift about a little on the rough rock, and again ponder our own curious motives. We have made the trip out here to enjoy, all right; but beneath that wish lies another: to connect ourselves to whatever goodness resides in the flux of nature. Our idle gaze, however, continues to fall on troublesome things—things that are beautiful yet curiously provoke doubt about that very beauty. What we glimpse of the working of causes behind phenomena disturbs our appreciation of flashing streams and swaying greenery, suggesting that we cannot entirely embrace the glories of the landscape until we have obtained some intellectual satisfaction. Such is the fickle mind! After long griping and urban moodiness we flee to the woods at last and proceed to think more critically than ever. The land is beautiful so it must be *good*, we reason; but the beauty, as it now seems to us, rides upon a flood of conditions and thus can have no stability, can promise no deliverance from rising and recurring miseries.

Feeling a little tired, although we have not really hiked very far, we manage to lie back gingerly on the rock and gaze up through the green hanging leaves, listening to the passing water. A life truly awake—what would that be? No troubles, with loveliness forever floating through our senses, all confusion banished—fine enough. But if there is still *cause* for troubles, if there is misfortune without remedy, if there is ignorance to generate confusion—how should we ever expect a paradise, or even an improvement in our present state? Oh, tiresome mind, will you not be at peace?

We wince and frown, then try to doze. Even with the rock slab so unlevel and rough, we might accomplish that. But now there comes to mind an embarrassing image of our own form sprawled listlessly here as if on a sofa, with closing eyes and disintegrating thoughts, daydreaming as on any lazy weekend. A life awake, indeed! So we haul ourselves upright again and try to stay alert. If there is truth to be found in perception then we had better perceive with some diligence.

Now as we look around us more deliberately we notice that, upstream and down, the creek is a rocky jumble, full of boulders of all sizes which must have come from the breakdown or erosion of ancient land. How much time was required to set these stones apart or to compose the whole picturesque arrangement? The massive inertia of change has worked upon the streambed countless ages before we appeared to sit and philosophize, and change will still grind on for ages after us. In this particular summer and in this propitious weather we occupy a fragment of rock, look around with fond eagerness, and experience a breeze of sensations that we call beauty. We are pleased, beguiled, and almost persuaded that nature is also *good,* that it in some way must operate in the interests of creatures, particularly us. But is it not rash to assume goodness where we feel, strictly speaking, only pleasure, refined and mild though it be? We need, beyond this, safety and assurance; but the stream, we cannot help but realize, does not flow for our benefit; rather it obeys laws, and races or dawdles according to impersonal conditions.

Just above the surface of the water we see swarms of small insects flying in and out of the shadows—a pleasant phenomenon, a visual amusement that we might squeeze into our theory of universal perfection—except that it unpleasantly occurs to us now that the tiny bugs are not at leisure and that something might very well attack them and kill them at any moment. Whether they have any consciousness of danger we do not know, but surely their restless state of existence, considered in itself, cannot be called secure. Meanwhile we who sit in relative safety on the rock might call these insects beautiful, might call the scene they contribute to beautiful— but can we reasonably ascribe any goodness or moral excellence to nature here? It is just our fortunate human birth that allows us, for the time being, to loll and sentimentalize; for were we so hunted we would hardly set such store by beauty.

The mortal repetitions of nature, the hunting and desperation and death, the blooming and withering, charm us only as long as we remain unharmed by them, as long as we can watch from a comfortable, aesthetic distance; but if we should fall and break an ankle, or step on a rattlesnake, or lose our way at nightfall, our philosophy would undergo sharp change—as it would, no doubt, with any number of diseases, losses, and failures, regardless of the loveliness of our surroundings. So why should we wait for calamities to disillusion us? Would it not be better to take up our perceptions with a more critical mind and dispense with timid evasions? Pain, hunger, and fear exist; they are common; they are normal, not exceptional; and they cannot be made to fit with our ideal of kindly nature, whether or not we wandering theorists are at present personally threatened. It is only by willfully ignoring suffering that we can preserve our picture of a golden, idyllic universe; once we acknowledge suffering at large we are driven to a more somber view; and once our own safety and peace are endangered, or once we have made the obvious inferences from natural facts, we must surely revise our philosophy.

Throughout the world creatures kill and suffer killing; everywhere there is error, bad luck, sickness, and exhaustion. For the most part this misery goes on out of our sight, which enables us, if we are sufficiently negligent, to dote on the benign displays of leaves, flowers, and moss, and contentedly admire the presumed perfection of things. But now that these prickly thoughts have stung us we feel unable to relax in that way and are moved toward more serious reflection. Is this philosophy? Is this meditation? Where is the warm tranquility we sought? What an irony that the surroundings we thought most conducive to peace should unsettle us as much as the city. Now we must work to obtain not merely tranquility but also the intellectual satisfaction that seems its prerequisite. Living creatures struggle and perish in inconceivable multitudes—we know it, so how shall we work the fact into our understanding of beauty and goodness? It is not a question just of pitiable animal multitudes, because our own human advantages are certainly temporary and unreliable, sure to disappear sooner or later and expose our common mortality. Would we regard our own disasters and the disasters within our families, when they come, as pleasantly picturesque, as necessary to cosmic beauty, as charmingly reflective of a lovely universe?

Huddled on this rock as the heedless stream swirls around it, we are feeling a bit lonely and, now that we think of it, even apprehensive. What sort of disaster could fall upon us this week or this year? And how can wildflowers and sunshine give more than a superficial balm? We cannot expect the hills and creeks to sympathize or even to notice our discomfort.

Some disagreeable conclusion seems to press upon us, and to avoid that we mentally thrash about for relief. Could we find something in the teachings of the Buddha to resolve the friction between observed danger and desired goodness? Buddhist history is full of stories of jungles, forests, and woodland retreats where determined monks and nuns lived in happy seclusion, where they struggled in meditation, where they sought and found the deathless *Nibbāna*. The Buddha himself attained enlightenment in a secluded, scenic place, and he recommended to his monks the advantage of a retired dwelling in the forest; however, he did not regard the beauties of nature as sufficient in themselves to precipitate liberation. There was as well the hard and frightening aspect of the wilderness, which he confronted during his search for enlightenment:

> Remote jungle-thicket resting places in the forest are hard to endure, seclusion is hard to practice, and it is hard to enjoy solitude. One would think the jungles must rob a bhikkhu of his mind, if he has no concentration....

I considered thus: "Whenever ascetics and brahmins
unpurified in bodily conduct resort to remote jungle-
thicket resting places in the forest, then owing to the defect
of their unpurified bodily conduct these good ascetics and
brahmins evoke unwholesome fear and dread. But
I...resort to remote jungle-thicket resting places in the for-
est as one of the noble ones with bodily conduct purified."
Seeing in myself this purity of bodily conduct, I found
great solace in dwelling in the forest.

(Majjhima Nikāya 4)

It was not any intrinsic goodness in the forest that brought the Buddha to his great achievement, but his purity of bodily conduct, verbal conduct, and mental conduct. After long self-discipline he had so weakened the obstacles within himself that the forest was no longer for him either a source of unwholesome fear or a sensory distraction but simply a congenial place in which to make the final effort:

Still in search, bhikkhus, of what is wholesome, seeking
the supreme state of sublime peace, I wandered by stages
through the Magadhan country until eventually I arrived
at Senānigama, near Uruvelā. There I saw an agreeable
piece of ground, a delightful grove with a clear-flowing
river with pleasant, smooth banks, and nearby a village
for alms resort. I considered:...."This will serve for the
striving of a clansman intent on striving." And I sat down
there thinking: "This will serve for striving."

(Majjhima Nikāya 26)

The striving—the intentional gathering of wholesome conditions and the abandoning of the unwholesome—is what matters most, and while the environment in which one does the striving may support or hinder one's efforts, it does not in itself supply any quality necessary for liberation. If it did, if liberation depended on external, worldly factors, then it would remain to some extent a fortuitous thing, not directly attainable. But such is not the case, happily for us. The Buddha emphasized that living beings are the owners and heirs of their own actions; they receive the results of their actions, good or bad. The purification of character, even to the point of complete liberation, is an individual prerogative and responsibility, not something to be left to the inspiration of accidental influences.

Such influences, be they pleasant or unpleasant, are often mistaken for moral qualities. On a fine summer day, after a satisfying lunch, in good health, and temporarily unpreoccupied with serious troubles, we stroll through woods or gardens and see the world as good—that is, as happy, obliging, trustworthy—when all that our experience really would allow us to say is that it is beautiful. The gratified mind infers too much when it assumes that whatever delights it does so out of a predisposition in its favor. Such unjustified inference leads on, moreover, to shock and grief when misfortune lights up the landscape with its glare. Then we are hit not just with specific pains but with a demoralizing disillusionment, when we find that what we thought good is not good, and perhaps never was. Death and sickness, failure and loss—how shall we smoothly account for them? Must we flee despairingly through the wreckage of our casual philosophy to the other extreme and bewail the universe as hideous and malevolent?

The Buddha describes all formations, all compounded things, as impermanent, and hence as *dukkha*, or unsatisfactory—a doctrine radically contrary to the common, conventional view of reality as fundamentally good or ultimately, if not presently, perfect. But to say that all formations are *dukkha* is not to say that they are necessarily hideous and malevolent; for *dukkha*, while it includes what is generally understood as suffering, also and more broadly refers to the liability to destruction inherent in all phenomena, their weakness, their variable, sure-to-dissolve nature. A particular phenomenon, or the world at large, might very well be beautiful, agreeable, and welcome to us on a given occasion without being eternally or categorically "good." Because worldly joy and pleasure do not last, cannot last, and must inevitably fade, they are, along with the gross miseries of existence, characterized as *dukkha;* but this does not give grounds for the pessimistic view that this universe is basically evil or hostile. Happiness and sorrow appear throughout sentient existence in varying concentrations, always depending on appropriate causes; so the obvious task for a realistic, pragmatic person is to diminish the causes for sorrow and cultivate the causes for happiness.

It is useless to extrapolate from specific pleasure to general rightness, or from specific pain to general malignity. It is far better to learn how benefit and harm both come to be and to set about improving our lives through intelligent action. This is exactly what the Buddha teaches. He advises us to observe how things arise and pass away, so that, understanding causality as the fundamental principle, we will be moved to pursue the good in the moral sense—not merely the aesthetic—and thereby benefit both ourselves and others. Although the flood of *saṃsāra* rages through time, although what is pleasant perishes, although pain and death assail all creatures, the religious-minded person may so comport himself as to strengthen his present equanimity, purify his mind, and eventually cross over the flood to the highest freedom of *Nibbāna*.

Working through these reflections, we have not noticed the world vanishing, and when we look up—for we find we have been brooding over the frothing, formless water in front of us—it takes a moment for the great amalgam of sight, sound, and all the rest to appear as something recognizable. Well then, here is the world again—stream and forest, boulders and sky, set around us just as so many elements variously combined. And it seems that another moment passes before we begin to be aware of the sensation of beauty. It too, we perceive, rises and falls, disappearing entirely when we are absorbed in something else. What shall we make of it then? When we have for the time being abandoned the fantasy of kindly solicitude in nature we are left with just the scented breeze across the stream and the worn boulders. Now we feel a certain degree of peace in this very plainness; and remembering that it is impermanent, not for our keeping, we simply breathe and blink and try to know the moment for what it is. It may be that, while forest, mountain, desert, and sea all rise and fall helplessly upon conditions, they yet present themselves to the watchful mind as scenes for contemplation, wherein what is beautiful hints at the yet unattained fulfillment, and even what is inimical or graceless supplies clues to truth. We need not believe that the shade of the tree overhead falls specifically for our comfort to be cooled and refreshed. We need not ascribe perfection to the drifting clouds to find the summer sky magnificent. We need not think ourselves unique or specially entitled, to hear with calm awareness the nearby birdsong and the water's gush and splash.

Is it time now for us to be moving? What pattern in the current or sensation in the body reminds us of the hour? We have not, to be sure, finished our adventure, and there is yet much work to be done in seeing rightly, guarding our impetuous senses, and acting in faith according to the Dhamma. Remaining in this world not really much longer than the gnats flying above the creek, we yet have the chance to set up the building stones of a free and noble character. If the splendor of a place unsullied by humanity awakes some gladness in us or lifts our minds to finer hopes, we ought indeed to make use of it—not in complacency, not in greedy grasping, but in detached awareness of the rise and fall of things.

The stream before us carries down the leaves, silt, and sticks of other regions, even as our intentional actions, the *kamma* we have done, pour through time to make the flood of our own sentient moment. Look there—more driftwood rolling past, submerged and rising. And there— what was that? We catch suddenly, or think we catch, a shocking glimpse of a furry, swollen mass borne along with the driftwood. Is it not some wretched creature dead and bobbing in the rushing water? We get up fast to look, but the ugly moment has already passed. If only we could detect quicker the brief revelations of the universe! We gaze after an imaginary spot, become lost, and then look upstream again, where on the next sweep of green water we see only innocent bits of seed-fluff gliding toward us and then away. We read what we will, admire what we will, but the stream bears all equally.

Now our sleepiness is gone. Good and evil, birth and death, fortune and misfortune ring out and rouse us. Should we not keep on exploring through the forest of contemplation? Perhaps the daylight will last some hours more and we may enter profounder landscapes. Now we step to the stream's bank, clamber up it, and get our balance once again on the trail. We hear the small sound of our breath as the noise of the stream drops away. Here is a moving body. Here are the speeding currents of mind, in which there flashes yet the intention to learn. All right, then, on we go with a determined stride as the scene around us changes. A bird twitches unseen in the foliage as we pass. Ahead, beyond huge oaks and beeches, the country dissolves in a summer blur, breeze-borne seeds fill the air, and worlds revolve with much withering and much flowering.

6
NOBLE STANDARDS

When we think of a holy person, an *arahant*, one who has attained full liberation, who is entirely free from the defilements of greed, hatred, and delusion, we do not imagine a particular physical appearance but rather a pattern of noble actions, a manifestation of poise, of serenity, of inspiring dignity. We imagine a way of speaking, standing, or sitting. Those inner qualities of saintliness must, to be meaningful to us, show themselves in behavior. It is behavior—observable conduct—which defines and exemplifies the true character of a person.

While we certainly have ideas, clear or vague, of what constitutes noble behavior, we are perhaps less sure of how that behavior is brought into being, how a person might actually come to conduct himself in a saintly fashion, distinct from the usual human course. Is it the case that someone first attains liberation and then begins to behave in an especially virtuous way? Is moral purity the incidental product of an abstract mental discipline? Might we simply apply ourselves to some meditative practice with sufficient energy, setting aside our moral deficiencies, until wisdom shall arise and by itself purify our conduct?

Such ideas are tempting, but wrong. There is no postponing good moral conduct, for it is just such conduct, even in tentative form, which makes possible the development of mental concentration and thence of insight or wisdom. Good moral conduct means, at its most basic, honorable restraint of bodily and verbal actions—the healthy, judicious self-discipline which must be practiced along with any kind of meditative exploration of reality. Furthermore, morality or virtue remains incomplete until it is extended to mental conduct as well. Because all this is difficult, because it goes against selfish interest, it requires specific attention and effort and a clear understanding of what actions lead to what results.

The Buddha taught that bodily conduct, verbal conduct, and mental conduct are each of two kinds—that which should be cultivated and that which should not be cultivated. The distinction can be seen in the results of each. Certain kinds of conduct naturally result in benefit, happiness, and well-being, and other kinds naturally result in pain and misery. It thus should behoove a serious-minded person to learn the difference between the two—which may easily be obscured by passion and delusion—and to strive for honor in action as well as in belief.

Within the Buddhist religion various customs, observances, rites, and formalities can arouse states of mind favorable for deep meditation and for compassionate behavior toward our fellow beings; but they do not by themselves produce spiritual advancement toward the supreme goal of *Nibbāna,* which is liberation from all suffering. Causality rules in matters religious as well as material. Misery and joy spring from particular causes, and mere wishing or mere performance of ceremonies cannot abolish misery and bring about joy. Any observant person realizes this principle to some degree, but what is less obvious is the extent to which even very solemn, dignified practices can remain decidedly superficial and ineffectual if not backed with virtue in daily behavior. The real good, the genuine achievement, always costs unglamorous, steady effort.

As a teacher of causality, as one who profoundly understood the complex of conditions behind painful and pleasant things, the Buddha was always intent on explaining how we should behave, how we should train ourselves in accordance with nature, so as to prevent the arising of evil and to promote the arising of good. There is nothing mystical in his method, no irrational reliance on luck, only a clear-minded instruction in worthwhile action. The spiritually dissatisfied person may reasonably try to rearrange his or her external environment or take up some observance such as chanting religious verses, performing devotional services, or practicing various systems of meditation; but none of these alone entirely remedies the fundamental disquiet, the *dukkha* born from craving in the midst of ignorance. It is not just what we determine to believe, as a theoretical, intellectual matter, that beautifies life; it is not even what formal exercises we do in the way of religious practice. The foundation—and the test—of all efficacious religious faith is the conscious adaptation of our daily behavior to noble standards. How do we deal with our family and our neighbors? What honor do we show in action?

We may be genuinely inspired by the ideal of spiritual liberation and sincerely decide to pursue it—but are we quite clear about what factors are necessary, or do we assume that throwing ourselves into meditation or devotional practice will itself take care of the details and accomplish the task? Liberation is possible; the overcoming of *dukkha* is possible—but only for those who go about it in the right way, not neglecting necessary conditions.

What then are the conditions to be gathered, or what are the proper actions to undertake? The Buddha summarizes the noble life as consisting of three "domains": virtue *(sīla)*, concentration *(samādhi)*, and wisdom *(paññā)*. These three, fully developed, lead to the destruction of sorrow and grief and the attainment of *Nibbāna* or ultimate liberation. Concentration may sound appealing, and wisdom even more so, but neither can develop properly without the foundation and continuing power of morality or virtue. The Buddha states the relationship explicitly:

> *Not possible is it, bhikkhus, without having mastered the domain of virtue, to master the domain of concentration. Not possible is it, without having mastered the domain of concentration, to master the domain of wisdom.*

(Aṅguttara Nikāya 5:22)

We must begin with elementary matters of conduct, for if these are undertaken properly they will help to bring about higher things. Actually, what at first seems elementary in the Dhamma may not be so at all—may turn out to be tremendously profound—and the careful student will remember that the Buddha taught and emphasized exactly what he knew to be good for living beings who suffer and long for an end to suffering. Every serious person recognizes the importance of virtue for a noble life, but perhaps not everyone realizes the way simple moral maxims in the Dhamma open up, spread out seamlessly into the grand pattern of spiritual maturity. Whether we are intent on the attainment of *Nibbāna* or simply hoping to calm our life and improve our character a little, there is a right way to behave—easily stated, but vast in its dimensions.

In the widest sense, the right way to behave is to follow the Noble Eightfold Path, which consists of right view, right intention, right speech, right action, right livelihood, right effort, right mindfulness, and right concentration. But to consider specifically fundamental moral behavior—what exactly we should avoid and what we should develop—we can examine the unwholesome courses of action and their counterparts, the wholesome courses of action. Certain kinds of behavior, because they spring from the unwholesome roots of greed, hatred, and delusion in the mind, are in themselves bad, unwholesome, and productive of misery; and other kinds of behavior, which spring from the wholesome roots of nongreed, nonhatred, and nondelusion, are wholesome and naturally beneficial.

There are ten unwholesome courses of action: killing living beings, taking what is not given, misconduct in sensual pleasures, false speech, malicious speech, harsh speech, gossip, covetousness, ill will, and wrong view. These kinds of misbehavior are always harmful, and when they become habits they lead the reckless person on to deep woe and misery in this life or a future life. They are the enemies of purity, the destroyers of peace, the bringers of trouble.

We prefer to think of troubles as coming from outside ourselves, as being imposed chiefly by fate, bad luck, the malice or foolishness of others, and so on; but in Buddhism we cannot dismiss our responsibility so easily. Through actions we have done in past existences we have been born in a particular situation in this world, with a particular mix of advantages and afflictions. Through a long series of intentional actions *(kamma)*, remembered or forgotten, we have in effect made up our own character into what it is today. According to our character, then, we respond to the surprises of fortune—we worsen situations or make them better. Often we feel helpless in the maelstrom of worldly dangers, but we should be sobered and encouraged by the Buddha's consistent teaching that actions have made us what we are, and thus actions—the conscious deeds we may possibly perform—have the power to make us safer.

Student, beings are owners of their actions, heirs of their actions; they originate from their actions, are bound to their actions, have their actions as their refuge. It is action that distinguishes beings as inferior and superior.

(Majjhima Nikāya 135)

Killing living beings is a form of unwholesome action with unwholesome results. When we intentionally kill or harm some creature, we perform an action, *kamma,* that has the potential to come back upon us at some point in the future. In countless passages in the Pali Canon we are advised to refrain from violence and to direct thoughts of friendliness and kindness toward living beings—both for our own good and for the safety of others.

Taking what is not given, or stealing, is likewise a fundamental sort of bad, unwholesome action. It too generates correspondingly bad results. Any person sensitive to his or her own welfare must reflect that the law of causality covers all intentional deeds. There is no succeeding in a theft, for such an action always plants a seed, whose fruit, in due time, can only be unpleasant.

Misconduct in sensual pleasures means specifically sexual misconduct— adultery, unfaithfulness, seduction, and sexual relations with children and other protected or helpless persons. To ignore the honor and dignity of others in the enjoyment of one's own lustful desires is categorically bad, wrong, and reprehensible. Such behavior proceeds from unworthy motives and creates future pain.

Four kinds of wrong speech follow next. The first of these is false speech—intentional lying. One who, when asked for the truth, deliberately lies plants an unwholesome seed which will bear unwholesome fruit. This sort of action is not only socially reprehensible but also, like the other wrong courses of action, has actual and significant consequences for the one who performs the action. Besides outright lying there is malicious speech—the deliberate attempt to harm someone's reputation or to cause dislike and aversion among people. Then there is harsh speech—all too abundant in the world and thus probably not taken seriously enough. It may spring from momentary anger or from a considered will to wound someone, but it is always, to one degree or another, an unwise and bad action. The fourth kind of wrong speech is simply empty-headed, foolish, idle chatter, which wastes time, provokes desires and aversions, and generally coarsens the mind.

These first seven unwholesome courses of action make up the basis of immoral behavior, that is, misconduct in bodily action and in speech. When indulged in sufficiently they may have very severe results, including rebirth in "an unhappy destination"—one of the wretched, painful planes of existence. It is the accumulation of one's good and evil deeds which determines the whereabouts and particular circumstances of one's rebirth after this lifetime. But even if one's evil deeds are not bad enough to generate rebirth in a lower world they can still have bad effects. In explaining the various kinds of evil action the Buddha says that the pursuit or habit of killing living beings will, at the least, cause a man to have a short life. Stealing the property of others will result in the loss of one's own property. Adultery will bring one "enmity with one's rivals." Telling lies will bring upon oneself false accusations. Speaking maliciously will cause "discord with one's friends." Using harsh speech will result in having to hear displeasing words in turn. Indulging in foolish gossip will "cause one to speak unacceptable words"—to give offense, to incur the contempt of others. These are all possible consequences of unwholesome behavior by body and speech.

The unwholesome courses of *mental* action—namely, covetousness, ill will, and wrong view—may also produce serious consequences. These courses do not refer to isolated, occasional bad thoughts but to habitual, built-up mental vices. Covetousness, the envious desire to get the property of others, and ill will, or cultivated animosity, are two mental attitudes which stimulate overt immoral deeds by speech and body. Wrong view means, in brief, the view that gifts and offerings do not matter, that there is no result to be expected from the good or evil actions one does, that mother and father are not significant, that there are no beings born into higher and subtler worlds, that there is no world beyond this one, that there are no virtuous sages who thoroughly understand the world. Wrong view is especially dangerous because adherence to what is immoral and rejection of what is worthy corrupt the mind, prevent the arising of wisdom, and cause one to fall easily into all sorts of bad bodily and verbal behavior. In turning one's back on truth and scorning virtue one puts oneself in serious peril.

The situation of living beings wandering through the uncertainties of *saṃsāra* is problematical already, and these ten unwholesome courses of action make it worse. They are the sorts of behavior that the Buddha says are not to be cultivated. What then should be cultivated? What better way of living is possible?

There are ten wholesome courses of action possible, whose nature is exactly contrary to the unwholesome courses of action. These are abstaining from killing, abstaining from taking what is not given, abstaining from misconduct in sensual pleasures, abstaining from false speech, malicious speech, harsh speech, and gossip; and avoiding covetousness, ill will, and wrong view. But how, we might ask, can abstaining or avoiding be considered a course of action? What positive benefit is there in not doing? The answer is that abstaining from misdeeds is not simply nonaction because the ordinary mind, misled by ignorance and other defilements, gravitates toward harmful behavior, and it is only a resolute action of will which can resist the tendency. To abstain from evil, then, is to exert oneself, to produce a positive moral force. One must have the alertness to see an unworthy deed for what it is and the will to turn away from it. The habit of doing this stimulates the growth of finer states of mind and results in rebirth in fortunate circumstances.

Furthermore, the thoughtful practitioner who abstains from bad behavior simultaneously trains himself in the cultivation of the good. Thus, while abstaining from killing, stealing, sexual misconduct, lying, and all forms of wrong speech, he generates good will toward living beings and consciously radiates thoughts of kindness and hopes for their welfare. Abstaining from bad mental conduct—covetousness, ill will, and wrong view—he fills his mind with generosity and detachment, with good will, and with the right view that good and bad actions do indeed have results and that there is merit to be honored and wisdom to be realized in this universe of moral law.

These forms of self-discipline by no means exhaust the domain of virtue. The Buddha teaches as well the principles of right livelihood, namely, that in earning a living we must be careful to do no harm to living beings—not deceiving, not cheating in the slightest detail, not grasping greedily for excessive gain. Furthermore, the Buddha counsels against indulging in the many sorts of folly and destructive entertainment available in the world. Many amusements may not be explicitly ill intended or distinctly evil in themselves yet may have the effect of destroying wholesome caution and making us more susceptible to bad impulses. Such distractions too should be avoided.

Virtue is also to be developed in small habits of consideration for the troubles and joys of others. Do we neglect our household or business duties in the offhanded expectation that others will do them for us? Do we see to our own comfort and only belatedly inquire after that of others? Does the pleasantness of our manner in any hour depend on how fully others grant our wishes or agree with our opinions? Courtesy or its lack may be a matter of custom, but as it both reflects and conditions our own minds we ought to take it seriously and strive for virtue right here in these ordinary, mundane moments. The innumerable problems, prizes, and disappointments of life continually oblige us to act and thereby to construct our character. It may be, therefore, that while we are impatiently waiting for a wonderful turn in our fortune or a sudden flowering of insight, our negligence or our humane attentiveness will actually be what we will have to stand on.

Virtuous thought and steadfast harmlessness despite temptation make it possible, make it easier for a person to act upon his or her best volitions and become better and worthier and as such a blessing to others. When intentions are carried over into virtuous action, one is superbly prepared to advance in the domains of concentration and wisdom. Without virtuous action, meditation becomes a rootless, lifeless thing, hardly distinguishable from any purely external ritual. Throughout the recorded teachings of the Buddha we find a powerful insistence on causality—how one factor gives rise to another and that to still another, and how, in the absence of a particular thing, another particular thing cannot come to be. When there is no effort made for purification of conduct by body, speech, and mind, there is no possibility of genuine happiness in this world, let alone the ultimate happiness of *Nibbāna*. When, on the other hand, such honorable effort is made—even when weak and tentative—mental development can take place and good things can follow.

It should be evident even from a brief look at Buddhist moral principles that what the Buddha aimed at—the ending of suffering—is not just a matter of practicing some religious observance or meditation with sufficient ardor. There must be a patient gathering of necessary conditions—and chief among them are these quiet, unprepossessing types of virtue. Cause and effect will tumble on with fear and sadness as long as we make no effort to hold to a noble course. What we *wish* for is a side matter (as everybody wishes for happiness). How, in the meantime, do we act? Out of the unwholesome roots of greed, hatred, and delusion there will arise, if we are not vigilant, unwholesome actions; and out of the wholesome roots of nongreed, nonhatred, and nondelusion there will arise, if we are diligent, what is wholesome and beneficial. If we exert ourselves mindfully and properly and if we are consistent in good conduct we will be able to achieve a true spiritual advance.

But in considering the power of intentional actions, we might still wonder whether, if past actions have brought us to this present reality and have constructed our present character, we are doomed to live out a fixed story, endlessly suffering the results of *kamma*. This is a common worry of anyone who starts to ponder the implications of *kamma*, but fortunately *kamma* is not responsible for everything that happens to us; nor is it infinite in result. If the past actions we have committed were to control everything, or if their results had to be experienced in exactly the same form and measure as originally performed, then there would be no possibility of a holy life; that is, we would be locked into a determined series of experiences forever and could not free ourselves from suffering. But this is not so. *Kamma* is, first of all, *volitional* action, intentional action; it is that which a sentient being consciously decides to do. Since volition is part of our mental makeup, and since we are always capable of undertaking new action, there is always the possibility of changing our overall character and fortune. We do not have, and never will have, the power to alter the restless universe entirely in our favor, but we are certainly capable of improving our individual situations through intelligent action, and of adjusting ourselves more healthily to this *samsāra*, which is naturally full of troubles and blessings, losses and gains.

Kamma, moreover, does not produce results with deterministic rigidity. It is not the case that a particular deed must give rise to a perfect reflection of itself at some definite point in the future irrespective of all other influences. Rather, *kamma* generates a potential which, in the presence of propitious conditions, will tend to ripen in a certain way; but conditions are constantly changing, each adding its influence into the stream of our existence, so there is no way for us to foresee an exact result of one drop or another. Actions are not isolated; they are interrelated and they condition one another in ways too complex to fathom. Throughout our lives we have perhaps done some good, some bad, and much we cannot categorize—all these are dynamic conditions in a dynamic and variable universe; and we can never unravel all the threads to the past or to the future. The Buddha in fact warns against speculation about the results of *kamma*, saying this leads to "frustration and madness." What we should keep before our minds is the mighty principle of causality—that over time we will become, we will experience, according to the way we have acted.

All our actions, furthermore, are of finite effect. Their painful or pleasant results appear and, whether they last long or not, they all subside in time. Therefore we should always continue to strive, by following a wholesome course, to reduce the bad and increase the good and thereby purify our conduct in body, speech, and thought, with the aim of eventually attaining complete deliverance from the instability of *saṃsāra*.

Everyone knows such work is hard. It is very tempting to neglect it, to keep only a minimum of decency (as we hurriedly judge it) and hope this will be enough to keep off guilt and perhaps even to progress in the domains of concentration and wisdom. Unperfected virtue, however, is not a static thing but a quality that varies with our actions; and given the impulses of the untamed mind we cannot expect that good states will automatically arise. The Buddha therefore advises continual effort:

> *I do not praise stagnation in wholesome things, monks,*
> *not to speak of a decline. It is growth in wholesome things*
> *that I praise, and not stagnation or decline in them.*
>
> (Aṅguttara Nikāya 10:53)

If our lives at any time seem serene, if we and our families are thriving, that is fine; that is cause to be glad. But the external conditions that make up good fortune are temporary and uncertain and far less trustworthy than internal, built-up virtue. Always we should exert ourselves to attain the higher good. The earnest cultivation of virtue is fundamental and essential, not only for the eventual attainment of liberation but also for our own protection here and now. The world being dangerous, we are sure to meet with some misfortune as it is—why should we open the door to more and worse through negligent behavior?

The Buddhist layman is expected to observe, at a minimum, five basic moral precepts: to abstain from killing, to abstain from stealing, to abstain from sexual misconduct, to abstain from lying, and to abstain from taking intoxicants; but even a little study of the Dhamma reveals that the moral domain is much vaster and that if we are really intent on our own welfare we should apply noble standards to all areas of our lives. Surely we would like to concentrate our minds better; we would like to acquire true insight; but how shall we do that if our conscience is always hounded by unworthy deeds or if we have never acquired a habit of self-control? We need, first of all, to cease doing unworthy deeds and then to train ourselves in ever greater alertness—not groaning pointlessly over past mistakes but cleansing ourselves with good behavior in the present moment.

This work, while not easy, is straightforward. Unlike the complexities of Buddhist philosophy and the subtleties of meditation, the components of the moral domain are readily comprehensible even to the beginner. This work also has immediate, observable application. What should be done and what should not be done are not just abstract, philosophical issues but urgent questions that arise constantly for everyone; they have to do both with the demands of mundane life and with our own deepest religious longings. Even without the aid of Dhamma we know inwardly that the moral choices we make will reverberate for a long time, so we hope to be able to make those choices without the apprehension that we are doing wrong or sliding into danger. And what if, beyond this, we could act with such confidence that our deeds would become not only a defense against danger but also a positive joy? With noble standards to trust in this becomes possible, for when we know that a particular deed is consistent with Dhamma and is aimed at the true benefit of ourselves and others, then we will feel satisfaction in carrying it out.

Kamma, we should always remember, is intentional action; so when we are in doubt about the morality of some action we are considering, or when we cannot find a rule that exactly covers the case, or when we have done something that has resulted in harm to others, it is helpful to examine our motives. Unintended actions are not *kamma*. No future suffering, no moral degradation, comes to us because of harm we have not meant to happen and have not tried to bring about. We are only responsible for what we directly intend and do. As long as we act with sincere good will according to virtuous principles we are acting correctly. Since the world is a snowstorm of contrary conditions flying this way and that, and since other beings are constantly doing actions themselves and experiencing the results of actions, we can never be certain that misfortunes will not occur for someone.

When, however, we become aware that on some occasion we have indeed intended and acted badly, violating a precept or otherwise behaving in an ignoble way, we should face up to the misdeed without evasion, recognize our mistake, and distinctly resolve not to behave that way again. Then we should go on with our business without unduly steeping ourselves in regret, which benefits no one. There is, when we look around us, always much good to be done, even in small, daily matters of courtesy and friendliness; and this sort of action, gladly undertaken, refreshes and elevates the mind.

Our duty is always to consider carefully and act as mindfully and honorably as we can. But we cannot stop here, because if we wish our deeds to become purer and more beneficial to ourselves and others we must observe more, learn more, contemplate more. The better we behave, the easier it will be for us to understand the Dhamma; the better we understand the Dhamma, the more we will be inspired to cultivate virtue. The noble person, the person of outstanding character, is the result of countless actions that he or she has done, countless efforts made according to noble standards. We ought not to think that we can govern all our actions with sheer improvisation, trusting to our supposed natural goodness. As long as desire and aversion burn and confusion and delusion gust across the mind we are liable to err and therefore should anchor ourselves to what is firm, to the Dhamma which the Buddha taught for our welfare.

Buddhist ceremonies, rituals, and observances have value insofar as they arouse and support wholesome states of mind; and these wholesome states, to be useful, must find expression in our overall behavior through body and speech. Periods of formal sitting meditation likewise have value when there is a genuine effort at developing wholesome states of mind. Admiring the ideal of emancipation or resolving to strive for it certainly gives worthwhile inspiration, but we must always have moral discipline to guide our striving. Any spiritual advance is accompanied by and indicated by worthier and nobler behavior—conscientious avoidance of bad deeds and performance of the good.

When we restrain and govern ourselves conscientiously, when we act with good intentions, we make it possible to establish right concentration. It is fortunately not a question of possessing some prodigious mental power but of putting the energy we have to work in the best way. Misguided energy, however strong, is useless; but energy that is controlled and guided by Dhamma can accomplish much good work. At its simplest, the concentration we need is just a steadiness of observation, a willingness to hold still, to gather our will and pay attention to what is happening for longer than our jittering whims would dictate. When the mind has such concentration it can see and understand things more clearly; that is, with insight; and eventually it is just such insight or wisdom which cuts off sorrow and opens the way to ultimate liberation.

Whether we are already eager to reach that liberation or only hoping for a little balance and peace here and now, the cultivation of virtue is a happy duty that should never be neglected. We might worry, we might complain that purity of action by body, speech, and mind is too hard to attain, we being fallible mortals with so many burdens and distractions and a lamentable history of failed resolutions. But we are not asked to perform heroic feats of abnegation. The work of Buddhist moral discipline is the practicable work that begins with reverence for what is honorable and pure and continues with many small daily actions. If we should ask ourselves, "Am I capable of saintliness today?" we would instantly say no; but if we ask, "Can I refrain, for this moment, from speaking out in anger?" or "Can I possibly give a friendly greeting to my neighbor?" we would surely have to admit we have the power for at least that much good. Then let us bring about that good, and we shall see what we can do next.

In one discourse, after urging the monks to abandon unwholesome things, the Buddha uses the same striking terms regarding the wholesome:

> *Develop the wholesome, bhikkhus. It is possible to develop the wholesome. If it were impossible to develop the wholesome, I would not say, "Develop the wholesome."...If this development of the wholesome would lead to harm and suffering, I would not say, "Develop the wholesome." But as the development of the wholesome leads to welfare and happiness, therefore I say, "Develop the wholesome, bhikkhus."*
>
> (Aṅguttara Nikāya 2:19)

Such development can be accomplished; it is not impossible; it is not beyond us. Higher states of virtue, concentration, and wisdom are attainable and worth attaining—that is why the Buddha taught the Dhamma as he did. If we find the Dhamma inspiring, if we think it can lead us to a nobler life, then we ought to follow it according to our power—which will grow as we determine to make it grow.

7
THE EMPTY VILLAGE

Early on this winter morning, as soon as we wake up, we become aware of a change in the universe around us. In the chilly gloom we hear a faint whistling at the nearest window. We rise and stagger over to look and find that a storm has overwhelmed the neighborhood. Outside we see the grand and terrible sweep of wind, with snow deep already and leaping and drifting in waves. The frosted window shakes, and a draft of icy air comes through. Houses and trees have sunk into fantasies in the feeble light, and even the dark, still room where we stand seems suddenly fragile, as if about to be overpowered by an immense reality. We go trotting about the house excitedly from this window to that, catching new angles and surprises of the snow-besieged neighborhood. There will be no work today, that is clear, no school, no smooth streams of automobiles, no comforting or anesthetizing routines, and perhaps (may it be so!) no stale thoughts.

A kind of fear or thrill is trembling within us as we pace around the limits of our dwelling, marveling at the power of the natural elements so suddenly revealed. It is unnerving to behold how tenuous our life and comfort are, but it is also inspiring in a strange way, as if the amazement of childhood has awakened once more. Maybe we have come to one of those dangerous junctures where the true character of existence with its harsh splendor breaks through the tedium of years. The snow pours, cascades, and whips across our view with astonishing velocity. The neighborhood around us is lost in desolate, freezing whiteness, and even the birds that yesterday enlivened the trees and bushes seem to have deserted this world entirely. The lights in houses are blurry, unsteady, and remote—so far away that they might be only memories of a former age. As we look out, our plans and schedules and conventions and habits lose their reality against the riotous cold. Everything has changed—what shall we do? Come then! It is time to stretch and inquire.

There is a rattling of the windows and a dire whistling around the corner of the house. In the basement the furnace rumbles dutifully, but we are not much reassured. How vast and ancient is winter, how furiously it breaks out of its brooding, how easily it obliterates warmth and order. Leaning close to the largest window, we observe the snow bouncing or sticking on the glass—gust on gust spraying in streams and fountains that load the sill and bury ever deeper the shrubbery and the now lost and frozen lawn. It is a calamitous morning with our solitude and frailty all at once made clear.

What shall we do but putter through these rooms (for there is nothing really to do) and come back to stand uneasily before the window, swinging our arms? We are ready to light lamps, build fires, cook breakfasts, and haul out blankets; but right now winter rants and no agitation in our household will matter much. We are, besides, fascinated by this wondrous upset of the ordinary. The storm has arrived suddenly with its huge negation of our importance, before which we can only squawk and gape. We imagine the wind accelerating and sweeping ice over all our amusements and pretensions. In any event, however the storm develops, we will not be consulted. We wait—as spectators, sufferers, astonished witnesses—without the power to still one breath of snow, while conditions surge and fall.

Within us, too, conditions surge and fall, and we notice elation, worry, and wonder in irrational succession. We feel a simple glee over the marvelous changes we see dancing across the landscape, and for a moment the storm is a thrill, a giddy adventure. But then we think about our work, our family plans, the supply of food in the house, the possibility of the electric power going out; and we listen more nervously to the furnace. Then in another second we are enchanted by a gray-and-white constellation of snow racing out of the distance to pelt against our windows. We seem to be looking at some fantastic illustration of universal destruction, and although we timidly suppose houses will keep standing and clocks and furnaces will keep working, we cannot help but shiver a little at the void so close upon us. The world without trembles, and the world within trembles in response.

But has this interior world of the mind ever been at ease, ever ceased to tremble? We notice now, at the instigation of the storm, the shuffling of fear, surprise, and planning; but is this inner turmoil really any novelty? Have we not, whenever we seriously inquired, come upon the same instability and disquiet? Within and without, nothing appears to have substance—we notice only an exhausting inertia. Perceptions, moods, emotions, ideas, and intentions rise one after another so fast—like sparks from a fire—that we draw back, startled and baffled, unable to distinguish beginning or end to the uproar. We cover this mental conflagration with the conventions of everyday life, and since everyone else is doing more or less the same thing—pretending the universe is acceptably tame—we get along after a fashion. But then there comes a storm, a misfortune, a calamity, and it becomes impossible to find any inner solidity to shield us against the outer flux. The more the storm blasts against our senses the more worried and excited the mind becomes. Faster and faster goes the motion of world and mind, until the very seething of it all paradoxically suggests a fearful emptiness. All is froth and turmoil; nothing stands firm. Beneath the teeming words, pictures, and fitful volitions what safe cohesion can we find?

Dizzied by the snow of thought, we have long gazed avidly upon the world as if to brace ourselves against fixed markers, orient ourselves by static stars. But whenever those stars or careless suppositions shift and reveal their own impermanence we find not steadiness but a greater emptiness. Gazing without wisdom on the inexhaustible landscapes of phenomena, looking for permanence, we end up searching a vaster nothing for a vanishing something. It is no wonder, then, that we lament and fear.

The snow that storms against the window reminds us of our physical frailty and our negligible defenses against ice and age. But out in those cold depths in the tumultuous wind, and in the depths of thought, we begin to glimpse as well a profounder truth. We have not found, and now hardly expect to find, any entity that stays unchanging amid the general dissolution. We have not found our self—or for that matter anybody's self.

The mass of habit that directs most of our life is permeated with a view of self, an assumption that within the storm of sensation and thought there exists, somewhere, an identity or ego that gives definition to experience and forms the core of our personality. We admit that the body changes; we admit that what we call the mind changes, too; but we have believed almost without question that a self within or apart from these exists as a particular, real, unique thing. Buddhism, on the contrary, dismisses our notion of self as nothing more than a way of speaking—a linguistic convention without substance. In explaining life Buddhism deals with directly observed phenomena, with the everyday sights, sounds, smells, tastes, touches, and mental objects that make up our reality. The imagined self or ego, because it cannot be viewed or grasped or indeed detected in any way, is irrelevant to the purposes of understanding reality and overcoming suffering.

Once we have at last begun to notice the perpetual elusiveness of the self we idealize so instinctively, and once we have begun to ponder the Buddha's declaration that all things are nonself, we will be prepared to act more consistently for the good, less hampered by baseless considerations. It is simply practical to set aside speculations about a self and examine that which is accessible, that which arises by way of our senses and forms the matter of our world. If we do this, if we fix mindful attention upon those things we can actually perceive, rather than those we only imagine, we can gather information that will be of material use to us. Since we live in a world of sound, color, smell, and so on, it is the direct knowledge of these facts which will enable us to act intelligently and safely.

The more we are absorbed in the notion of a personal ego the less capable we become of promoting our own welfare through wise action. The Buddha teaches that our intentional action—*kamma*—generates results for us both in this life and beyond. When that action is born from greed, hatred, and delusion it will tend to ripen in suffering. Self-absorption, self-conceit, and self-praise, no matter how heartfelt, how ingenious, do not promote our happiness in any way but merely thicken the clouds of delusion; therefore for our own good we must go against the wind of habit and try to look objectively, not subjectively, upon the world. The truths we need to nourish us are found right here in the working of the senses.

Gazing through the window into the depths of the snowstorm, we observe great gusts and currents and even, with some concentration, the individual flakes that give them such substance as they have. Conditions infinitesimal and uncountable build and fall everywhere. Millions of icy specks assemble the snowdrift that the mind summarizes in a glance. Conditions pile up, too, to make a tree, a human being, a world; but because these conditions are all impersonal, transient things, empty of intrinsic identity, the perceived objects they bring about must likewise be impersonal, devoid of ego. We who peer out through the cold glass also belong to the category of things that change. We are snowdrifts heaped by the countless actions we have done.

What shall we call this state of things? The Buddha calls it impermanent, unsatisfactory, and not self. Such a reality is a mass of unstable conditions in mutual dependence, and neither in general nor in particular does it offer us anything we can call substantial or durable. Thus, despite its immensity and variety, the world is rightly seen as empty of any ego. It is known to us through our senses and for all practical purposes is inaccessible apart from sense perception. Venerable Ānanda, the monk who served as the Buddha's personal attendant, explains that our view of the world and of ourselves is a product of the various kinds of perception and the organs of perception:

> *That in the world by which one is a perceiver of the world, a conceiver of the world—this is called the world in the Noble One's Discipline. And what, friends, is that in the world by which one is a perceiver of the world, a conceiver of the world? The eye...the ear...the nose...the tongue...the body...the mind is that in the world by which one is a perceiver of the world, a conceiver of the world.*

> (Saṃyutta Nikāya 35:116)

Perceiving various phenomena by eye and ear and the other organs, we conceive ideas, construct opinions, and suppose pictures of reality. Basically what we deal with, what we reason upon, is not some independent, self-supporting, self-contained entity within, and not some indubitable, objective world without, but rather these countless events or instances, these perceptions of visible forms, sounds, smells, tastes, touches, and mental objects, out of which the "world" comes to be. These perceptions are the blizzard in which we stagger and get lost, for we continually grasp at this or that snowflake in the hope that it will prove substantial and trustworthy. But neither alone nor together do these specks of sensation give us the certainty we wish for. They are empty in that they have no content, they bear no weight, they vanish even as we gasp with wonder.

There are, the Buddha teaches, six internal sense bases: eye, ear, nose, tongue, body, and mind; and there are six corresponding external sense bases: visible forms, sounds, smells, tastes, tactile phenomena, and mental phenomena. But neither within nor without can we fasten on anything of absolute solidity and permanence. None of the sense bases give lodging to a self. When examined they are found to be empty, devoid of true comfort.

> "The empty village": this is a designation for the six internal sense bases. If, bhikkhus, a wise, competent, intelligent person examines them by way of the eye…ear…nose… tongue…body…mind, they appear to be void, hollow, empty. "Village-attacking robbers": this is a designation for the six external sense bases. The eye, bhikkhus, is attacked by agreeable and disagreeable forms. The ear… the nose…the tongue…the body…the mind is attacked by agreeable and disagreeable mental phenomena.
>
> (Saṃyutta Nikāya 35:238)

There is this "empty village," this collection of sensory organs which, though complex, is uninhabited by any entity. Through the ear, for example, the perception of sound occurs, but it is like the reverberation of a gong—the brass trembles from an impact and gives rise to a metallic boom but itself knows nothing, understands nothing, merely responds and relapses into silence. Cause and effect waver through the gong, and through the human ear, but the internal sense base, like the responsive metal, holds no intrinsic truth, holds nothing we could rightly call a self.

Eye, ear, nose, tongue, body, and mind are "attacked," moreover, by their corresponding objects, both agreeable and disagreeable; for what those objects cause—looked at realistically—is disturbance, irritation, and excitement of one sort or another which, in the presence of ignorance about the nature of reality, stir up desire and anxiety. Empty physical and mental processes endlessly succeed one another: when sounds collide with the ear a certain kind of consciousness—hearing consciousness—arises. It is likewise with visible forms and the eye, odors and the nose, flavors and the tongue, tactile phenomena and the body, mental phenomena and the mind. Through the interaction of impersonal conditions, consciousness continually flickers into existence and then fades away.

Outside the window right now there is indeed much flickering and fading—in the minute flecks of ice that cluster momentarily on the glass before skittering away. Things appear and, almost before we can register the fact, vanish—so if we are going to call them real we have to admit that this reality does not have the solidity and permanence we would like to believe in. The storm is an exception, an aberration, perhaps, in the ordinary succession of events, but except for its violence it is not fundamentally different from the daily rise and fall. Here we see the transience of perceptions that make up the world for us.

Staring like this into the snowstorm, we begin to feel a kind of frustration, as if we were being buried under a drift of abstractions or illusions. How can we ever get through to what truth exists? The winter daylight has fully arrived now, but only to show more mysteries in the snowfall and further vistas of wilderness. How, if it is possible at all, can we contrive to live wisely in the midst of such flux? Seen thus, the storm overwhelms us—but only while we are trying to found a life on what by its nature cannot hold up. The snow will not obey us—we cannot direct the multitude of snowflakes to settle down neatly here or there just as we would like. Our senses will not obey us, either—we cannot adjust them to perceive only what is beautiful or pleasant. When an external phenomenon falls upon the internal sense organ, the ownerless process of perception is launched; and if it goes one way when we have wished it to go another, certainly we will suffer, certainly we will feel helpless and overwhelmed. It is the idea of ownership, the idea of "my" perception, which bewilders us. All we can really be said to "own" is our intentional actions, and our actions can never control the greater universe around us.

If, however, we do not seek our peace or fulfillment in that which is beyond our power to arrange we will not get lost in storms of frustration. The sensations that appear to us are ultimately not ours at all but only empty phenomena that function according to impersonal conditions. If we cease to grasp at them we will cease to suffer from their waywardness.

The *arahant*, the enlightened person, experiences both pleasant and unpleasant sensations, but the *arahant*, no longer deceived by the illusion of self, knows them as mere sensations, mere conditioned things empty of identity, and lets them go by without worry. It is precisely in dispassion toward these that security is found. The ordinary, worldly person supposes that he must scoop up huge quantities of pleasure, while dancing away from all dangers and pains, for life to be considered secure; thus he struggles, strains, and of course fails, because his senses cannot help but reflect the variety and unevenness of the objects that reach them. He glimpses the endless upheaval of the universe, is shocked, and strives to make it other than what it is, not realizing that what is beyond his reach can never be made to respond to his desires. But one need not be an *arahant* to adopt a wiser course. If one understands in principle the conditioned nature of the senses and their objects one can behave in such a way that delusion is decreased.

The Buddha calls this behavior "noble restraint of the faculties." While the world at large seems to encourage a ravenous indulgence of the senses, the rightly practicing follower of the Buddha restrains, guards, and disciplines his sense faculties:

> On seeing a form with the eye, he does not grasp at its signs and features. Since, if he left the eye faculty unguarded, evil, unwholesome states of covetousness and dejection might invade him, he practices the way of its restraint, he guards the eye faculty, he undertakes the restraint of the eye faculty. On hearing a sound with the ear.... On smelling an odor with the nose.... On tasting a flavor with the tongue.... On touching a tangible with

the body.... On cognizing a mind-object with the mind,
he does not grasp at its signs and features...he undertakes
the restraint of the mind faculty.

(Majjhima Nikāya 27)

This restraint is accomplished through mindfulness *(sati)*, which observes calmly and neutrally the arising and the passing away of phenomena. It is not a question of squeezing shut our eyes and ears to prevent disturbing perceptions from occurring, but of making sure we do not seize upon and cling to those perceptions, because grasping after what has no firmness opens us up to unwholesome, damaging states of mind. Mindfulness shows us clearly what is happening in the present, flickering moment—so that we will not be so tempted to stuff ourselves with emptiness, so that we will detect harmful tendencies before they get a hold on us, so that we will be able to stand against the flood of conditions.

Many sorts of sense objects, we should remember, are decidedly dangerous to us because they particularly give rise to greed or aversion or other harmful things; they pound upon our weaknesses with a fearful power. Therefore restraint of the faculties is called for. By vigilant mindfulness we can keep the load of stimulation manageable—recognizing these perceptions as the empty things they are, considering their impermanence, taking note of their dangers, acting or refraining from acting with judgment, on our own initiative. In such a way we protect ourselves from the onslaught of painful passions.

From our perch on the sofa, with the great storm playing out in front of us beyond the glass, we see limitless instability; and perhaps after a while we are inclined to wonder whether, if all phenomena are so empty and weightless, we need bother with mental discipline in the first place. Why not shrug, dream, drowse along as well as we can? And anyway, even if we admit that such restraint of the sense faculties might indeed be prudent, maybe it is simply too hard for us. Do we really need to attempt it? There is, it seems, only one way to resolve the questions. Shall we pursue it?

Now we are moving, freshening our thought with bodily action, whimsically smiling. Is the snow unreal? Is the world unreal? Let us see. At any rate let us have a quick look at the weather. With a heavy coat on our shoulders and boots on our feet, we are soon ready for a quick experiment. We pause for a moment, fumbling belatedly for some mundane excuse to go out—to check the depth of the snow or see if a snowplow is on the way or something just as pointless—but happily our inspiration carries us onward. We touch the front door tentatively. It is cold. We open it—and instantly a shocking gust of wind hits us, spraying snowflakes into the room. With a gasp we stagger out onto the porch and close the door.

At once the household warmth is lost to us. It is still snowing and the wind is racing and stinging, making us duck down and turn away from it. We stand undecided on the porch, blinking against the snow, trying to remain aware of the excitement in our senses. The world is white and gray, incoherently streaming. The porch with its glittery covering of snow does not seem familiar to us; nor do the wavering houses in the distance. The street is an emptiness without tracks. We cannot distinguish between the snow now falling and the snow blown up from the drifts, for it all comes rolling and spinning in freezing gusts. We see nobody else, only the blurred, scarcely real shapes of houses and trees; and it now occurs to us that we behold an "empty village" like that of our own vacant senses, against which the "village-attacking robbers" of wind and snow charge. It seems strange, terrible, and wonderful that a simile spoken in unthinkable past time should suddenly break out of imagination into the tremendous here and now. We turn a little, amazed, squinting into the distances. What were we going to look for? Everywhere snow is blowing, sticking to the tree limbs and streaming off again.

The stark landscape, the hiss of the wind, the snow biting our skin— these are the present facts we cannot reason away. Now without the sturdy window to hold off the truth, without the leisure of the house, we cannot find any beauty in the storm. It all flies against us; or perhaps it flies through us, irrespective of us—numberless conditions in headlong rise and fall. So if we are quite irrelevant to winter's business, might we not, for our own good, try to raise a moment of mindfulness? Perhaps there is something worth attending to right here in the body's shivering, here in the audible scratch of snow at our ears or in the light that leaps into our eyes. Something might be done with this; knowledge might be found.

And that restraint of the sense faculties—might it be possible to be calmly aware, without grasping or aversion, of the minute fluttering of nature and of the stormy rise and fall of all perceptions? We stand as steadily as we can, looking out across this new wilderness, ready just to notice experience as it happens.

The huge, hollow world blows on without end, and we are too cold for any romantic appreciation of the storm. Our senses are functioning; we have no doubt of this; and real or unreal, these perceptions are sharp enough! This must be why we should restrain our senses; for although these sights and touch sensations and all the rest are empty things, they yet will sting us or enchant us; they will lead us, if we are negligent, into delusion and misery.

A moment more, while a loose gutter rattles somewhere above us— and we are chased off the porch by the terrible wind. All right, that's enough! We must heed the conditions of the moment; so we retreat, getting hold of the icy door latch, shoving the door open, slipping inside, heaving it shut again with a bang. Out of that wind—enough of that! We stand shivering, sniffling, shaking the snow off in a world suddenly narrowed and made still.

Now we must try to slow down a little, to reassemble a predictable life. Soon we have our boots off; soon we are hanging the coat on a hook— but we still feel cold, and even now all these tame objects in our dwelling place seem mysteriously invested with something of our own excitement; or else we are guessing at the great dynamism and emptiness within all forms. Our walls are so thin, our roof just a tissue in time. What a wonder how things arise and vanish!

But as storms are impermanent, too, perhaps we need not despair, if we retain our mindfulness. Perhaps we might outlast this upset in the elements, and, if so, the reasonable thing, the human thing, is to go on with our duties. Within the great disorder of winter might we not make some small order for our own good? Let us—for example—have our breakfast. Sense objects arise and pass away indoors, too, and in the smelling of toast and the tasting of jam we can notice the same sequences by which the whole world becomes known to us. If we would know it truly, we must guard these sense faculties as the Buddha teaches, so that covetousness and dejection may not break in to wreck our understanding.

So we eat, sitting at the kitchen table with our little arrangement of silverware and plates, while the furnace keeps us warm enough. We feed the body; we conduct this small ritual to sustain a thinking life, to affirm our human hope, even in a way to transcend the blizzard through attention and self-discipline. After we have finished—taking our time while the outer winter does what it will—after we have carried the dishes to the sink and washed them and set them in the rack, we turn to the window again and observe, without great surprise, that the storm is dying down. The wind fades; the snow comes slower, without excitement, dropping straight, trailing away at last to nothing. It is like the ringing of a gong, which booms and drones and dwindles until at some undefinable point the sound slips out of the present and into memory.

So in time the storm slides off. The sky drags over all the whiteness without a sound. But in a while, as we gaze and wonder, we are roused from abstraction by a sudden chirping and scratching at the window. There on the sill two or three sparrows hop, spin, and flutter, scattering the snow about. They too have lived through the storm. What inspires them in all this cold? We lean to look, but in an instant they are gone, answering no questions, zipping over the landscape toward the limitless sky.

8
A LIFE OF WORK

The practice of Buddhism should not be thought of as something apart from daily life, as a kind of spiritual recreation or intellectual retirement from all mundane needs and duties. Rather it is a way of living rightly at all hours, in accordance with nature. We do need periods of silence and quiet reflection, but we also need a mindful attitude toward the mass of tedious and busy time that we struggle through every day. A truly contemplative life should be one of attention, energy, and work, informed by an understanding of what is wholesome and what is unwholesome and what is worth pursuing and what is not.

We usually look at the laborious and unexciting parts of the day as time to be gotten through, put up with, endured in the expectation of more pleasurable, worthwhile moments. But life, considered at large, is mostly ordinary and unremarkable, the indisputable joys being relatively rare and brief; so we find ourselves in effect casting off, pushing aside, despising the greater part of our time. Even if we incline toward contemplation we might treat it as another kind of special pleasure, to be sought after we have suffered through the demanding hours of duty. Work, we suppose, is one thing and religion quite another.

In Buddhism, however, we do not find any such division of the day into tedium and recreation, or material cares and spiritual leisure, or hours to cherish and hours to reject. True improvement in our lives is not just a matter of more minutes allotted according to desire, but of wiser attention and worthier behavior at all times. Since most of us must spend many hours in work, study, errands, household chores, and care of children, we need a way of carrying out these duties with the least trouble and, if possible, the most spiritual benefit. Work well performed does not have to be mere blank time, a miserable subtraction from the substance of our life, but rather a chance to develop spiritually even as we attend to the most mundane of requirements. The teaching of the Buddha is always aimed at the removal of suffering and the promotion of happiness, and we find within it not only the theory and technique of higher mental discipline (what we call, somewhat loosely, "meditation") but also practical advice on matters of work and home. Whatever our religious or philosophical hopes, we must make a living. How shall we do that according to good principles?

In teaching about right livelihood the Buddha explains that we should not make a living by any form of trickery or dishonesty. If wealth comes as a result of our energy and diligence, that is fine, but it should not be sought out of avarice, or obtained by lying, cheating, or deceiving anyone in any way. Moreover, right livelihood is a form of livelihood that does not inflict harm, pain, suffering, or death on living beings. A particular trade might be profitable or easy or otherwise convenient and congenial, but if it would oblige us to deceive or harm others it is not a proper trade for us to follow. It does no good to excuse ourselves on the grounds that we are just making a living or just providing for our families—we are still responsible for our own intentional actions and will be the heirs and recipients of the effects of those actions.

Any serious, thoughtful person should look further than the material desires of the moment for guidance in behavior. It is necessary to provide for our families, but this can be done without violating moral precepts and without causing harm to others. It may be difficult; it may be less remunerative; but it is possible, and in the doing, in the honorable undertaking of harmless work there is a moral profit, a moral benefit both for us and for our families that will last a long time.

Assuming that we avoid harmful or deceitful occupations, we are quite free to do whatever work we like. Buddhism does not recognize any particular worldly occupation as being inherently superior to the others in moral quality. Some professions enjoy greater income and greater public esteem than others, but we do not advance ourselves spiritually simply by pursuing this or that profession. The most important distinctions are distinctions of individual behavior: how do we carry out our work—with or without diligence, courtesy, honor, faith? Whether we work as a clerk, a teacher, a mechanic, a homemaker, an engineer, or anything else, we must, to be free of remorse and worry, fulfill our duties honorably.

If, then, we manage to avoid unwholesome actions and the worry connected with them, is there any more spiritual benefit to be obtained from work or must work simply be endured? We would like to think that work should not only provide us with our necessities but should also constitute a deep and satisfying pattern of activity, one that consistently gives us the feeling of accomplishing something meritorious. This is a pleasant idea, but how far it can actually be realized is uncertain. Modern society offers so many forms of employment, so many ways of making a living, that we readily assume there must be some job possible for us which will fit perfectly with our desires and talents and will give us both income and enjoyment; but life is usually not so convenient, and whatever occupation we take up has its annoying drawbacks. Instead of constant pleasure, we meet with fatigue, boredom, frustration, and disappointment more often than seems proper. Have we made a bad choice of a job after all, we wonder, or is there a way to approach the work which will turn it into the source of joy we have hoped for?

While there are fortunate people who thoroughly delight in their work, they undoubtedly are not thrilled and inspired every day and are certainly not immune from common troubles, frustrations, and sorrows; so we ought not to feel especially deprived if we cannot find a job filled with purpose and happiness. It would be more useful to ask ourselves what, given present circumstances, is possible and practicable for us in the way of making a living. We want honor, wealth, recognition, and general gratification, of course, but realistically, setting aside fabulous luck, what should we be looking for?

First of all, we should recognize that much of the work we must do throughout our lives is simply not chosen; it is just the natural accompaniment to our social and familial relationships. We have to take care of our children; we have to prepare meals; we have to keep our houses clean and comfortable. It would be entirely fanciful to suppose that all this could be done with delight. Furthermore, even those appealing jobs which, theoretically, can be chosen, may not be quite complete in their advantages, or free of disadvantages and onerous requirements. We often find that, instead of obtaining the ideal, we must out of practical necessity go to work in some other field, or accept a less desirable position. This is just the way things go in this unstable universe, and a mature person realizes that disappointments can never be entirely avoided.

Much of the misery connected with work is the result of excessive expectations and impatience with the naturally imperfect conditions of *saṃsāra*. Since we work, fundamentally, in order to make a living, we ought to consider what exactly a "living" should consist of. We must get adequate shelter, food, and other necessities for ourselves and our families. We also need, on a subtler level, the exercise of our faculties, the healthy stimulation of our minds, and the emotional reward of accomplishing necessary tasks. Beyond these factors desire may, and does, expand infinitely, causing problems to expand as well. As in all worldly endeavors, if we rely on changeable, ungovernable phenomena for our happiness we must be prepared for plentiful misery as well, and to the extent that our requirements increase we can expect the difficulty of satisfying them to increase also. The world offers innumerable potential pleasures, amusements, pastimes, and possessions which, with sufficient means, we might obtain; but is the effort to obtain them a natural, reasonable part of making a living? The answer to this will vary with our individual, subjective views of what is important; but clearly, if we are hoping for our work to enable us to get fine, expensive things, we are reaching farther than we actually have to for the maintenance of life and health.

The universal complaint is of being too busy, too harried, too pressed to enjoy in the way we presumably should enjoy. Working, racing to achieve things, we perennially fall short, fall behind, lose time, and accelerate all the more until our higher purposes become lost in the struggle to cope with the demands that rain upon us. We strain so, we believe, because the job requires it, because the family depends on us, because this is the price of a satisfying form of work. But how much satisfaction do we actually get, and of what quality? And how far have we thought out the requirements of genuine contentment? Many forms of employment require arduous concentration and constant readiness; and we might be up to such challenges; we might consider them worthwhile; they might bring welcome gains. But if we recognize that the busyness is in fact too much for our health and peace then we ought to step back and reflect not just on what kind of job we should be doing but also on what we revere and value most—what goal or ideal deserves our faith.

This is a religious question, and for the Buddhist or for any deeply serious person the religious question must come before all purely mundane decisions. A good parent, relative, or friend is not adequately defined by the worldly status of his or her occupation, for those persons we most love and admire and remember are those of noble *character*, those who possess such virtues as kindness, wisdom, patience, and faith. To become a worthy person in the highest sense is to behave, to train oneself in such a way that unwholesome qualities are progressively abandoned and wholesome qualities are developed until the mind is pure and at peace. If, then, such an ideal appeals to us we ought to make sure that our means of livelihood does not conflict with it or distract us from its attainment.

Busyness is not necessarily diligence. It may be only a way of coping with fear or lack of spiritual purpose. We may seem very energetic, active, and capable to others, but if we notice that unwholesome qualities within us are increasing and wholesome qualities are decreasing we may be sure we need to revise our habits. This in fact is a very important principle throughout all of Buddhist teaching: that the value of an activity is best gauged by what sort of results it produces in the mind. Do good mental states appear, or do bad? Are we inspired or demoralized? Let us learn this before we approve or disapprove.

Some of our busyness and agitation comes from outside demands, from the sheer pressure of wound-up modern life, but much of it comes from our own desire—that timeless force that knows no noble goal but only the object of the moment. We wish to obtain and hold on to pleasant things, and this requires, it often seems, a sacrifice of quieter satisfactions and a dedication to unslackening mundane work. In order to reach a certain level of affluence we might have to forgo much that it is vital and refreshing—is this truly to our advantage? It would be wise at least to consider that if we are willing to make do with less we might keep and even increase other blessings.

Undisciplined appetites and ungoverned busyness do not make for a fulfilling life; but Buddhism does not by any means recommend the other extreme of idleness or indolence. We are enjoined to fulfill our duties honorably, maintaining our households, managing the finances of the family carefully, guarding our children, and helping our friends. Sloth is a hindrance to the correct development of the mind, and the Buddha always advises his followers to strive, to exert themselves for the attainment of the good. If we wish to have any stability at all in our fortune we must take care of both material business and mental development.

The realm of work extends—or should extend—beyond home, office, shop, and factory into the mind itself. There is, in this difficult human plane, the constant necessity of making a living in the material sense, but there is also the necessity—less obvious but just as urgent—of working for the purification of our own minds. This is a kind of labor which is not forced on us by the world but which we undertake as we gain faith in the Dhamma and understand what harm may follow from our negligence and what benefit may follow from our diligence. Rightly practiced, the spiritual life is not a respite from effort or a dawdling in abstractions but a conscious exercise of our faculties, a determined striving for the destruction of suffering and the establishment of happiness. Since all phenomena within *saṃsāra* are conditioned, produced by causes, it is important to examine those causes and work to remove the causes of harm and establish the causes of benefit. This is practicable work, valuable work, which includes and reaches beyond what we usually think of as our job, occupation, or livelihood.

One of the functions of Buddhist monks and nuns is to exemplify this spiritual work in a comprehensible, inspiring way, so that people will look favorably upon the teaching of the Buddha and be moved to apply it seriously in their own lives. To work for an ideal quite apart from worldly profit and fame is sufficiently unusual in this hurrying world as to puzzle many and raise useful questions in the minds of thoughtful people. It may indeed seem that the Sangha, the monastic order, does not work at all, that monks and nuns, being mendicants, merely depend upon others; but a closer examination reveals a restrained, disciplined, and diligent ideal of life which, if practiced as it should be, results in peacefulness and steadiness. The Buddhist monk, it is true, does not work at a job, is not employed in the commercial sense, and is bound by his disciplinary rules to depend on the gifts of lay people for his basic material needs; but his conscientious, full-time labor for spiritual goals makes him a true worker.

The Buddha himself always emphasized the virtue of supporting those who sincerely followed the path of renunciation, because such generous, wholesome action will certainly bring blessings to the donors. It is recorded in the Pali Canon that once a supervisor of plowmen was distributing meals to his workers when the Buddha, carrying his alms bowl, came near and waited. The supervisor said, "Ascetic, I plow and sow, and when I have plowed and sown I eat. You too, ascetic, ought to plow and sow; then, when you have plowed and sown, you will eat." To this the Buddha replied that he too plowed, sowed, and ate; and when the man said that he did not see him plowing, the Buddha responded thus:

> *Faith is the seed, austerity the rain,*
> *Wisdom my yoke and plow;*
> *Shame is the pole, mind the yoke-tie,*
> *Mindfulness my plowshare and goad.*

> *Guarded in body, guarded in speech,*
> *Controlled in my appetite for food,*
> *I use truth as my weeding-hook,*
> *And gentleness as my unyoking.*

> *Energy is my beast of burden,*
> *Carrying me to security from bondage.*
> *It goes ahead without stopping*
> *To where, having gone, one does not sorrow.*

In such a way this plowing is done
Which has the Deathless as its fruit.
Having finished this work of plowing,
One is released from all suffering.

(Saṃyutta Nikāya 7:11)

Hearing this, the man was impressed and immediately invited the Buddha to eat, acknowledging him as a true plowman. A diligent life, we should see, is not limited to material labor alone; and it is right to recognize and respect the worthy labors of others.

Worldly work, when conscientiously attended to, brings worldly benefits of various kinds, while the strenuous work of virtue, concentration, and wisdom that the Buddha accomplished, and that he taught to his followers, bears fruit in the "Deathless," or liberation, emancipation, *Nibbāna*. Yet we should not assume that these two kinds of work are opposed, or that only one is possible for us. Even though we may be engaged in full-time employment and numerous family duties, we should remember that the Buddha taught the Dhamma for the welfare of all beings and that the Dhamma is not something that can be practiced only under special conditions of leisure or within the discipline of the monastic life. Rather, the Dhamma can and should be made part of our hours of work, study, leisure, and all. It is a matter of developing an observant, mindful attitude toward what we are actually doing in the present moment.

For example, much of our time goes to repetitive chores—washing the dishes, folding the laundry, cleaning the house—which we usually try to get through as fast as possible while our minds frantically anticipate the next duty on our list or loaf about in daydreams. It is true that our time is limited, but it is still possible to make more out of these familiar moments. Why should we glumly let so much of our lives drain away without giving us any spiritual refreshment? Whether we are setting the table or painting a wall, we can pay attention to what we are actually doing—to the immediate physical actions, to the appearance and disappearance of perceptions and thoughts, to the succession of intentions and small actions that make up the work. The discipline of meditation is basically a systematic attention to the processes of mind and body and all of nature; and as these processes are going on all the time we might exert ourselves a little to see what they can tell us about reality. The universe displays its nature everywhere for whoever will train himself to watch, to notice, to contemplate how phenomena endlessly arise and pass away. This is a means to knowledge, and also a means to tranquility, for the better we perceive this swift and universal transience the less susceptible we will become to pointless excitement.

Even during more demanding activity it is possible, and extremely useful, to set up and maintain mindfulness, because mindfulness, in addition to giving us valuable information about reality, helps us to accomplish our work efficiently. When we are well concentrated on the present moment, paying attention to our actions, we do not waste time; we see the requirements of our tasks more clearly and are thus better able to apply our skills properly. Moreover, the exercise of mindfulness reduces mental agitation and distraction and promotes calm, so that work, while it might not be made entirely pleasant, is at least relieved of extraneous affliction.

The work of mental development, like mundane work, is fruitful when it is carried out intelligently, with clear understanding of which causes will lead to which results. We might possess much enthusiasm and energy, but if we exert ourselves in the wrong way or mistake danger for advantage or fail to resist unwholesome factors, we cannot expect happy results. The Buddha tells us that greed, hatred, and delusion are unwholesome and not to be cultivated, while nongreed, nonhatred, and nondelusion are wholesome and worthy of cultivation. Our actions—and hence our future—arise out of these roots, so it is vital to distinguish the unwholesome from the wholesome and then strive to expel the one and increase the other. In this work there is no reliance on luck—just a sensible confidence in the process of cause and effect, whereby things come into being when the necessary conditions are present.

The jobs, businesses, or professions we engage in have their uses and benefits: they bring wealth, knowledge, and the satisfaction of skillfully exercising our minds and bodies. To work regularly is for most people a necessity, so it will be an additional, spiritual benefit if those hours of labor, through steady reflection, can be made to earn insight as well as money. If we take good care of our material needs we gain a feeling of maturity and capability that will help us to achieve higher things. If we see for ourselves how in earning a living certain causes—diligence, reliability, effort—give rise to certain effects—income, prosperity, satisfaction—we may be emboldened to use the same principle in reaching for spiritual blessings. At the end of the week, when we believe we have rightly earned our pay, when we have finished our share of work with confidence, we might well consider that such effort, such striving, ought not to conclude with just these worldly attainments, for we do not, surely, live just for them. They make life more pleasant; they fulfill our duties to our families—but all prosperity remains incomplete without the attainment of a pure mind. Such mundane pleasures and comforts are impermanent and thus not ultimately reliable. Therefore, should we not, as we carry out our daily responsibilities with honor, devote some conscious effort to the development of our minds?

Sometimes, perhaps, at the end of a day of work or even an hour of ordinary chores, when fatigue is not too great, when we have confidently settled present problems, there comes a subtle feeling of peace and rightness. It is not exactly the accomplishment of any specific, temporal task that then pleases us but rather the rare sensation of gliding in a quiet world, as if for the moment we have found the smooth course on which we belong, where suffering recedes from consciousness and equanimity arises. Such a feeling never is won by thought alone, never is just willed into being, but instead occurs out of a complex of intentions and actions. We work, we apply body and mind to the prosaic moment, and when intention is firm and we finish putting in order some small necessity, we realize the fitness of our effort—how conditions flow, for once, without bewilderment, bringing peace that we wish would last.

Here the attentiveness and energy of ordinary work pass over, it may be, into the sublime work of Dhamma that gathers noble conditions for a noble end. Such rare equanimity, though it vanishes swiftly, may teach us to step onward, with a more definite aim, into the practice of systematic contemplation. Intuition urges us, and the Dhamma we have studied confirms and guides the intuition. The rightness we have felt might be made sure and realized more fully.

Liberation from suffering is worth pursuing. For this the Buddha taught the Dhamma. We twist one way or another to reach for phantom happiness, but eventually, when we learn the futility of grasping, when we pay heed to the timeless Dhamma, we must admit that liberation is the noblest goal. The ending of suffering and the attainment of ultimate happiness are exactly the same thing, which may be realized through noble work.

9
SPEECH AND SILENCE

When we arrive at work in the morning or when we happen to see our neighbors across the lawn or at any time when we run into an acquaintance, the desire to speak usually arises in us. At the least, we feel that it is courteous to exchange greetings. Then we may have business to accomplish or news to exchange or simply some general good will we wish to express. Ordinary speech, if not always delightful, is easily released and serves at least as a diversion or relief from boredom. We speak not just to convey or solicit information but to amuse or to find amusement, to avoid loneliness, to attract attention, and to demonstrate our willingness to belong to the social world. Even when we are alone speech still concerns us, for we spend much time considering the nuances of what we have heard and planning our own requests and complaints. What persuasion can we put into our words, what explanations can we make? Such is the influence of speech on the listener and on the speaker that it is not surprising that the Buddha considers speech an important aspect of conduct that must, like bodily actions, be properly governed both for amicable relations with our neighbors and for the ultimate attainment of liberation.

It is not hard to grasp the general meaning of what the Buddha designates as wrong speech: false speech, malicious speech, harsh speech, and gossip. But keeping aware of the hundred daily impulses toward such speech and restraining ourselves are for most of us much more difficult. Furthermore, with what are we to replace wrong speech? Given the irritations of life and the demands (internal and external) we must deal with, what can we say that will be both honest and useful? Is there such a thing as speech that is not only harmless but also positively beneficial for our spiritual development? And besides the moral quality of our words, do the actual subjects we talk about have particular drawbacks or advantages? And, in the midst of so much worldly din, how far should we determine to talk at all?

To speak, discuss, or communicate in any way is to perform an action, and all intentional action generates a potential for future results for whoever does the action. We know that ill-intended words can wound, deceive, or otherwise harm others, whereas kind and amiable words can comfort, educate, and encourage; so no great insight is required to recognize the wisdom of purifying our habits of speech for the welfare of others and our own future tranquility. But a general appreciation of the ideal of right speech is seldom enough to make us speak wisely in ordinary social interchange. Too often what we think right to say is only what the desire or aversion of the moment urges us to say. If we pause to review our motives and the requirements of the situation we may be able to stop or soften wrong speech, but even then we may not know exactly what, if anything, should be said. It is certainly to be hoped that we can catch ourselves before uttering damaging words, but it is also to be hoped that we can learn to speak in a way that brings about good, even when nothing requires us to do so.

Each of the four kinds of wrong speech has its beneficial counterpart. A person who is sincerely trying to practice right speech refrains, first of all, from speaking lies for his own benefit or that of anybody else. Moreover, he sees to it that when he does speak what he says is true, straightforward, and reliable. In any group or assembly, when asked to tell what he knows, if he does not know he says so, and if he does know he explains that too, factually and honestly. The principle here is not only to refrain from technically speaking falsehood but also to try faithfully to say what is true.

The serious practitioner also refrains from speaking maliciously, from passing on rumors, from slandering, and from trying to produce division and disagreement. He is, as the Buddha says, "one who reunites those who are divided, a promoter of friendships, who enjoys concord…a speaker of words that promote concord." Such a person aims at supporting general good will through discreet, peaceful speech. It may be tempting to pass on unflattering information that will cause division among those we dislike or envy, but if we are to live up to the standards of right speech we must try to refrain and instead to speak in a way that will make for peace.

The fatal human tendency to speak harshly causes so much obvious misery, resentment, and strife that we can hardly doubt the wisdom of refraining from this sort of speech; although in practice most of us find it very hard. Too often we react to life's normal or exceptional annoyances with angry, cutting speech. Later, perhaps, in cooler reflection, we regret our rashness; and if we can thereafter watch over ourselves more closely that is certainly to be counted as progress. But even if we manage to control ourselves fairly consistently we are still not doing all we should do until we undertake to speak the opposite of harsh speech; that is, "such words as are gentle, pleasing to the ear, and lovable, as go to the heart, are courteous, desired by many, and agreeable to many." We may find it hard enough just to clamp down on our anger in speech, but the Buddha would have us extend ourselves so much farther. This might seem too hard except for the fact that gentle, courteous, and friendly speech, while it certainly soothes the listener, also soothes and pacifies the speaker, so that the underlying anger is diminished and made more manageable. Restraining the unwholesome and promoting the wholesome are thus complementary, mutually strengthening efforts.

Likewise the fourth category of wrong speech—gossip or idle chatter—has the two aspects of restraint and development. The Buddha advises us not to gossip, not to indulge in pointless, trivial, useless chatter. Such talk, besides wasting time, lowers the quality of our thought and keeps us from the valuable work of observing the world with mindfulness. Who can really hear or see when he is chattering on about trivial things? But apart from the customary gossip of the world, what else, we might wonder, is there left to talk about? The Buddha says that one who practices according to Dhamma "speaks at the right time, speaks what is fact, speaks on what is good, speaks on the Dhamma and the Discipline; at the right time he speaks such words as are worth recording, reasonable, moderate, and beneficial" (*Majjhima Nikāya* 41). Encouraging, inspiring speech is both welcome and useful amid the often dispiriting babble of human society, but such speech requires thought and consideration beforehand. The serious practitioner, then, should think and consider and then speak "at the right time" on serious, substantial subjects. To inquire, to discuss, to propose ideas, to draw others' attention—and one's own attention—to the Dhamma is to speak rightly and to do good.

Unlike time-filling gossip, meaningful, animated talk about the Dhamma does not stupefy, does not distract, does not blur the senses. When the purpose is kindly and when the subject is virtue, concentration, or wisdom, the attentive mind is nourished, revived, inspired to better effort. The Buddha originally taught the Dhamma, we should remember, because he knew that it had the power to elevate and to liberate and that if people had the chance to hear it and if they practiced it they would be able to make progress toward the elimination of suffering. Thus we should try to replace pointless, idle speech with speech concerned with Dhamma, both for our own good discipline and for the well-being of others. When we speak of worthy things, moreover, we give others an opportunity to respond in kind and in fact to help us with their own experience and ideas.

The sphere of right speech thus extends past the basic requirement of abstaining from evil. Speaking sensibly and listening to sensible talk educate us and lead us on to further mental development. As always, it is a question of cause and effect, of conditions giving rise to other conditions: we are formed in part by the words we hear, and when we hear and pay attention to good and meaningful words, inspiration and faith tend to follow. Thus the Buddha advises us to seek the company of wise and virtuous persons, because it is among them that we are most likely to hear edifying speech that will encourage faith. When there is faith founded on sound reason and inspiring example, there will be a stronger will to carry on with what is right.

It may be that on some occasion we suspect that what we have to say, even though well intended, may not be welcome. Should we speak or keep silent? Here the answer will depend on whether or not it is possible to do any good in the particular situation. When asked by Prince Abhaya whether he would ever say anything unwelcome and disagreeable to others, the Buddha asks him what he would do if he saw a child putting a pebble or a stick in his mouth. The prince says he would hold the child's head and remove the object with his finger, even if it hurts the child, because he has compassion. The Buddha then explains that he, a *Tathāgata*, does not use any speech that he knows to be "untrue, incorrect, and unbeneficial"—whether or not it is agreeable or disagreeable to others. Speech might be true and correct yet at the same time unbeneficial; and that too the *Tathāgata* does not speak. Then there may be speech which is true, correct, and beneficial, and which may be either agreeable or disagreeable to others. In these cases, "the *Tathāgata* knows the time to use such speech. Why is that? Because the *Tathāgata* has compassion for beings" (*Majjhima Nikāya* 58).

These are reliable principles to follow. We should try always to speak honestly, accurately, out of worthy motives, when we perceive that our words will have a good effect. Thus critical or sharp speech is permissible if it is true, correct, and beneficial. A parent may certainly admonish a child, or a teacher a pupil, or a friend a friend, if he or she speaks out of a wish for the welfare of the other. With both agreeable and disagreeable words we must, as the Buddha notes, know the time; that is to say, patience and tact are necessary, along with a calm understanding of the situation and the personalities involved. The factor of right speech does not require us to blurt out everything we are thinking about someone, but rather to discipline ourselves wisely so that when the time is right, and when we do decide to speak, our words will be worth listening to.

When it is obviously the wrong time to put in our opinion, or when we simply do not know what to say, or when there is no reason to talk except to add to the general din, it is better to keep silent. The Buddha discouraged the monks from indulging in idle, worldly talk, and told them that when they assembled they should either speak about the Dhamma or maintain a "noble silence." For the Sangha, which is charged with studying and practicing the Dhamma and representing the Dhamma to the world, a very high standard is required so that others will be inspired and supported in their faith. Poise, dignity, serenity, and other good qualities need a certain quietness in which to flourish— a silent time in which to observe, to reflect, to gain strength. To make too much sociable noise, to be constantly raising one's voice for attention, is to waste time and to neglect meditation. When no words are called for, or when enough talk has been exchanged, a noble silence is a wise refreshment.

Monks are not expected to maintain perpetual silence or cultivate taciturnity for its own sake but rather to speak or keep silent with a graceful manner, depending on the needs of the moment. When there is nothing useful to be said one remains quiet and mindful; when there is business to be done one talks business; when there are visitors to welcome one speaks in a welcoming way. The Buddha himself customarily engaged in courteous and amiable talk with those who came to see him and spent much time advising and encouraging them. Following his example, we should fear neither speech nor silence but should know when each is suitable and not take up the pointless agitation of the world at large.

Whether we speak or refrain from speaking, we should supervise the intentions that move within us, for they determine the quality and effect of our actions. Then too, what we choose to talk about and what emphasis we give to it influence our own personality in good or bad ways; and then according to our developing habits we continue to speak and thereby to fortify those habits. For example, the Buddha says that an ignoble or untrue man will readily reveal the faults of others, whether or not he is asked about them. Being questioned and given an opportunity, the ignoble man speaks "without omitting anything, without holding back, fully and in detail." As to the praiseworthy qualities of others, however, he is reticent; he does not volunteer praise, and if he is questioned he will speak only incompletely. Regarding his own faults the ignoble man is not inclined to speak, or if he must speak he does so "with omissions and hesitatingly, incompletely and not in detail." Regarding his own praiseworthy qualities, however, he speaks "fully and in detail." Such a person, the Buddha says, should be considered an ignoble man.

The noble-minded man, the true man, by contrast, remains discreetly silent about the faults of others or, if he must speak, says little. But he readily praises the praiseworthy qualities of others, not needing any request to do so. He readily admits his own faults, speaking of them fully, not minimizing them. About his own praiseworthy qualities, however, he has nothing to say, or if he must speak he speaks of them "incompletely and not in detail" (Aṅguttara Nikāya 4:73).

From this we can see it is not only the tone or technical accuracy of what we have to say that counts but also our intentions regarding ourselves and others. What exactly do we wish to impress on those who hear us? If we would wish to be known as noble-minded, or, better, if we think we should actually *become* noble-minded, we ought to discipline our intentions and actions honorably. Right speech is speech that is true, not false; friendly, not malicious; mild not harsh; and meaningful, not gossipy. It is also speech that is judicious, tactful, and generous. One who is devoted to such speech steadies himself in the storms of social life, where balance is rare and where sensible, nourishing words are often drowned in the roar of craving and aversion. To speak kindly, with dignity, of important matters is to benefit both oneself and others; it is a way of behavior that arouses further good qualities in the speaker and in the listener. And on occasions when no speech is necessary, keeping a noble silence is beneficial, because it allows one to listen and it gives others the opportunity to speak thoughtfully in turn.

There is, as it happens, much of meaning even in this chaotic world which can be profitably listened to in noble silence. Above all there is the counsel of virtuous persons—which in youthful haste or adult distraction we perhaps have neglected. If we slow down and listen attentively we may hear sensible words that teach us what we must develop to reach spiritual maturity. There is also the ordinary speech of society, the day-to-day matters of work and friendship which, though seldom explicitly concerned with religious questions, still express to the sympathetic listener the ancient human longings for truth and peace. Through conversation, laughter, complaints, and busyness, *saṃsāra* continues, and the facts of impermanence, unsatisfactoriness, and impersonality may be contemplated.

Then too, there is speech of a kind in the animal world all around us. Stepping outside our house in the morning, we hear the birds crying and the summer insects clicking and trilling, adding depth and richness to the world. Everywhere a kind of communication goes on among creatures, and while we may not be able to extract a literal meaning, we may at least sense, if we contemplate carefully, the common stir and longing, the universal restlessness of conditioned existence.

Even in what is without speech or without intended meaning we may find spiritual nourishment and wordless education. Above our conversations wind flutters through the maple tree, unobtrusively reminding us of *samsāra*'s restless change and our own unfinished search for liberation. At night the rain thumps on the glass of our window hour after hour. By day the growl of automobile traffic rises and falls. Electronic chirps and the rattle of machinery surround us. Footsteps come and go. Laughter, words, gestures, and symbols fly through our senses—briefly present to be contemplated, if we wish.

When we keep noble silence we have the chance to observe without excitement how the world really operates, how cause and effect make up and break down the patterns of phenomena. When we observe in this way, quiet and alert, what began perhaps just as hypothesis or interesting doctrine takes on power in direct experience. Formations change before us, illustrating, repeating, reinforcing the Buddha's timeless words. We hear expressed in the speech of other beings our own wishes and fears, so that we are made more aware of the common suffering and the need to conquer it. We hear also in the incidental noise of nature and society the same conditioned processes that run on without any goal of their own. Must we forever drift through spells of pleasure and pain, never getting wholly free from *dukkha*? Not only words, not only sounds speak to the concentrated mind, but all mindfully observed phenomena that rise and fall. If in a noble silence, a sensitive quietness, we contemplate these things at length we tire of drifting and gather motivation and conviction for progress toward freedom.

Silence helps us to learn how defilements of mind result in suffering and how virtues result in benefit. We begin to see how the factors of the Noble Eightfold Path combine and support our hope. Reflecting on the teaching of the Buddha and pondering the world before us, we should realize how vital right view is for beneficial action. After the quietness of thought and observation we should see how important it is to speak rightly, and how we should strive with right effort to abandon the unwholesome and cultivate the wholesome. Throughout the universe, in all good or evil matters, insight or ignorance will produce effects; one action will make another of the same sort more probable—and out of these our future is constructed. When we begin to speak, therefore, it should be as another considered, wholesome action proceeding from a right view of reality. The factors of the path work together, as the Buddha explains:

> *Therein, bhikkhus, right view comes first. And how does right view come first? One understands wrong speech as wrong speech and right speech as right speech: this is one's right view.... One makes an effort to abandon wrong speech and to enter upon right speech: this is one's right effort. Mindfully one abandons wrong speech, mindfully one enters upon and abides in right speech: this is one's right mindfulness. Thus these three states run and circle around right speech, that is, right view, right effort, and right mindfulness.*

> (Majjhima Nikāya 117)

As baffling and overwhelming as *saṃsāra* is, there is a right way to behave which will lead us to safety. We must understand our situation; we must make an intelligent effort with mindfulness; we must control ourselves in speech and all forms of action. What, after all, is really within our reach? Just this mind and body. Most of the universe flies past, heedless of our will, but these can be tamed, and their taming will help us toward the emancipation we have needed so long.

Taming our speech is just part of our task, but we should not neglect it; for here is an essential means of restraining the bad and promoting the good. We should remember the epochal effect of the Buddha's own speech—for it was by speech that he offered the incomparable Dhamma to the world, by speech that he encouraged and inspired his followers. Speech has great power, and when speech is guided by wisdom it can do enormous good.

The easiest course, the negligent course, is to let words burst out in automatic reflection of every stirring of resentment or craving; but this will do no good for us or anyone else. When, on the other hand, the mind is informed, educated, and brightened with right view, speech becomes easier to control. When speech is controlled the mind in turn is lightened— made that much freer from disturbance. Thus good effects accumulate and make for spiritual progress.

Whenever we wrestle down the urge to lie or otherwise to misbehave in speech, or whenever we willfully speak good and honest words, we help to purify the atmosphere in which we live, we lessen troubles, and we climb a little closer to emancipation. Daily, by will and word and action, we go on making our own destiny. How shall we complain that we have no power? What words are we preparing now to release? Right speech is part of the Noble Eightfold Path. Everyone who wills can fulfill this duty and experience a deserved satisfaction.

10
A Procession in Sunlight

On this shining autumn afternoon practically without wind we are attending to errands on a busy street, trotting along in absent-minded good humor. Such a golden light falls out of the measureless blue heavens that even this stretch of ordinary sidewalk seems, for the moment, entirely satisfactory. We are getting our exercise, going from one unimportant place to another with a cheerful appreciation of the weather and the scenery. This is one of those suburban collections of shops and restaurants and offices, a nicely kept-up block with maple trees at intervals, stirring agreeably with business on an afternoon so light and trivial it seems not fixed in time at all but murmuring on through eternity. We have a few more things to get done before we can go home but they do not worry us much—a brief appointment here and there, a stop for this and that. It is enough that we feel healthy and are able to hurry down the sidewalk with a casual interest in the color and movement around us.

We pause on a street corner, waiting to cross the street to our next stop, breathing placidly, feeling the sunshine through the still air as the traffic streams idly by. But down the street there—what is that? We see a car approaching with its headlights on—no, a line of cars—and we note, in our light, mild mood, that it is a funeral procession. On it comes without haste down the colorful, bustling block—a black-and-chrome hearse and a couple of limousines, followed by ordinary cars, regularly spaced. We dawdle on the curb, counting the oncoming lights. There are maybe a dozen cars in all, probably headed for the cemetery just up the road.

Nothing unusual. If there must be a funeral, we reflect, it is a fine day. The maples are brilliant, the air tranquil.

We wait patiently enough as the hearse rolls toward us, rolls by slowly, slowly, but without pause. And then come the gleaming limousines, coasting easily through the golden afternoon. Through shadows and reflections we glimpse the mourners within—formally dressed people sitting straight, not speaking, being borne along quietly according to custom through the middle of the busy world. They go by—men and women in the silence behind the glass, hardly distinguishable figures with thoughts incomprehensible and far from ours, distant shapes which will be gone into the past before we have drawn more than a couple of casual breaths.

But now we glimpse, between the glaring flashes of sun on the windows, one figure in a limousine (a woman? a man?) not straight at all but bowed over, hand to forehead, bent in an attitude we suddenly and terribly understand. We do not expect this in the cloudless afternoon with the appetizing smell of food around us and music mumbling faintly along the sidewalk and sunshine everywhere light and golden. We do not expect to see such a figure bent with feeling among the other self-contained and solemn figures behind the shadowed glass. And now the afternoon that hitherto has flowed on in normalcy is torn by death and human tears. That stricken form in its timeless, prophetic pose speaks to us silently through the glass, over the rush of the limousine—and all at once our blitheness is gone and we are looking, it seems, at no single person but at a universal figure that tells without a word what it is to lose, to be bereft, to grieve.

It is as if time has gaped open here and inflicted truth on us. Behind the conventional and the customary, the raised, ineffectual hand and the bowed head bespeak the mortal pain we fear and have not escaped. We would have all sorrow distant and brief, ended with a ritual and fanned away by music; but now with the containing glass grown momentarily transparent we are not separated from the mourners and cannot pretend to indifference. Whose body do they follow? What husband, sister, child, mother, lifelong friend? What sudden decease or weary, long expiring? And now what tormented love that reaches and finds nothing?

Into a street of cheerful busyness the funeral procession intrudes with bleak dignity; into our airy thoughtlessness it intrudes as well, heavy, slow, and irresistible—symbol of the solemn reality beneath our sparkling after-noon. While we joke with the clerks in stores, while we bustle onward with this or that to do, with a mind of pleasure floating loose, that pro-cession moves on somewhere with someone else's grief; and now it is here and passing; and soon enough we too, stunned to quietness, will ride in that procession, sit straight or bend, and find the vivid world pale. Now we are chastened to behold that universal grieving figure; we are con-nected to the grief and sorely reminded that we have never, for all our joys, danced beyond its reach.

We remember now, do we not, how once in a while such a procession has cut off our path, balked us, warned us, set us back a little? But we have detoured always; we have put off, put away the obvious contemplation. Shall we now turn aside again? Shall we stare with determined thought-lessness at the sky and wait until danger vanishes? Soon indeed our abashed plans will twitch back to life and we can hurry on in health and confidence—with one more vision fended off, one more mystery avoided.

But we cannot, it seems, quite choke off this instant's knowledge. Gold sun notwithstanding, the afternoon is darkened as the indistinct, mourn-ing figure glides past us. Glass and steel slip away fluidly, leaving behind a turbulence of reverie as other, past deaths now flood through our mem-ory. All those relatives and friends, those lives we knew! Never in the past was there freedom from death, and not now, either; and with death always undealt with, unremedied, how shall we not bow over, too, in grief and fear, when it comes next to us?

The procession rolls by with momentary gleams of headlights, rolls on away from us—and then the break in the afternoon's smoothness is closed. But we are left now strangely outside the sunny scene, unsteadied and isolated by memory on a forlorn street corner. For so long we have assumed the right answer to grief or to fear was diversion—the facile dodge, the hasty plunge into work and play—but now, though our eyes are again importuned by colors and our ears by music, we are not diverted, we are not drawn away to dreams.

While the traffic accelerates easily in the clear sunlight we loiter on the sidewalk, sensing endless depths of time and suffering. However we pre-tend, life still founders, sinks away to recollections; and all the comforts of old times disappear. We patch our hopes up and make do, flee into busyness; but there is no escaping the procession of impermanence. Can we ever cease from evasion and turn to face it? The more we try to stamp our claims on the world the faster the marks seem to fade. Can we ever live without conceit and fear?

The fire of *dukkha*, the burning unsatisfactoriness beneath all vain exertions, bursts into our consciousness, then falls to smoldering, then flares again for reasons we have not understood. We suffer and then, when misery subsides a little and pleasure revives, we manage to forget. We know we should work to shun evil, build virtue, and act for the good with clear intention—but how can we keep our minds to that work when the world so beguiles, when we can almost believe the placid autumn's reassurance?

First of all, let us maintain a good thought when it comes. There is work we should do to free ourselves from suffering—we will acknowledge this readily enough—but how shall we go about it? Among the recorded teachings of the Buddha we find five simple, accessible truths which he advises everyone—monks, nuns, lay men, lay women, all—to reflect on frequently. The contemplation of these five things stifles the fires of conceit and makes possible the earnest cultivation of the good. Shall we make the effort to consider them in this effortless afternoon? They are easily stated, not hard to remember:

> We are sure to get old.
> We are sure to become ill.
> We are sure to die.
> All that is dear to us will change, disappear, depart;
> and we will be separated from all of it.
> We are the owners and heirs of our actions, and
> whatever good or evil we do will assuredly be our
> inheritance.

If we would bravely know the dimensions of our human plight, here they are. These five reflections, seriously practiced, weaken the tendency to run heedlessly after pleasure and to become self-satisfied and complacent. The world with its limitless enchantments deceives those who forget fundamental realities, so if we wish for an undeceived, independent view we must take care to notice the actual conditions within which we live and strive.

At first look, these conditions are decidedly not pleasant, and it is hardly surprising that our minds, already agitated, should shy away from such revealing contemplations as the Buddha recommends. But there is a great deal of benefit here, so we ought at least to give some thought to these matters which touch us so profoundly.

If we calmly reflect, "I am sure to get old," we are considering not a theoretical possibility but what is true, what is a certainty for living beings. Amid the sea of illusions, of guesses, of doubts, of possibilities, this stands out, stands true—not a good thing, not a pleasing thing, indeed, but a reliable sign by which we may direct ourselves in worldly turbulence. Old age, we know even now, will undoubtedly bring more limitations on us who fear limitations, and quite possibly new and strange forms of suffering; so how shall we deal with those disturbing conditions? Contemplation of our coming old age will rouse us to do the moral and spiritual work we know we should do.

But now as we pace about on the sidewalk in the vivid, sunny autumn, we wonder how we can reflect on old age with any urgency when perhaps we do not, right now, feel old at all. Perhaps we are still young in years and see the future as gloriously elastic and distant; or perhaps we are not young but have such fortunate vigor and energy as prevent us from envisioning a time of serious frailty. It may be hard to imagine this active, flexible body slowing down, weakening, failing to turn and skip with the freedom that so pleases us now. But if our imagination is lazy, the senses that we turn so eagerly upon the surrounding tumult of life can show us sobering signs. Let us look around mindfully—what do we see, what could we see, that we have hitherto let pass unremarked?

An innocent autumn scene surrounds us—but in a moment an uneasy thought or two floats up, and then we have to admit to ourselves with a kind of shame that we have seen and do see important signs. On our walk today, not two blocks back, did we not stride by the entrance to a building where a few elderly people stood about or sat on a bench in the sun? It is a nursing home, but as we know no one there, and are usually absorbed in our errands, we have sailed by—one time or twenty—without a thought, missing what is real as we grope through dreams. But there, sitting quietly in the sun or going in or out on the arm of someone younger, is the form of our future. If we would know what old age is should we not slow down a little and think? And if we fear old age should we not reflect all the more until we have come to terms with it?

The second reflection taught by the Buddha follows relentlessly upon the first. We are sure to become ill. There is no doubt about this, either— but with what rashness do we plan our days, ordain our future, assuming the body will always painlessly leap up to do its work! The occasional ill- nesses we have suffered so far in our lives still seem to us anomalies, aber- rations in the physical universe which ought not to recur at all, let alone get worse. We understand that grave disease, injury, and incapacity are possible, but as we do not see any reason they should happen to *us* we briskly go on counting on permanent health. The foolishness of this is obvious, but we might not resist the foolishness unless we have energeti- cally educated ourselves by reflection on the certainty of illness.

And again, as with old age, we need not have illness immediately crush- ing us in order to ponder this truth profitably. There are signs, there are instances to be noticed in our own families, among our friends, and all about us. What, again, have we neglected on our afternoon jaunt? Look- ing above the bustling shops and offices, we now see what was there all along—the great bulk of the local hospital that stands behind and above the street. True enough. We must admit it—symbol and fact stand every- where, as brilliant in their own way as the autumn maples we thought- lessly admire. Up in that high building, in many stark rooms, weariness and pain are more than theoretical. There are long, uncomfortable silences. Many sighs are breathed. Someone sits even now, perhaps, at one of those distant windows and looks out, looks down with a slow, considering gaze on all of this—and with thoughts how different from our own!

This also is our destiny—to lie and listen to far-off sounds, to sit up, lie back again, blink at the ceiling, dream of health. The bolting will is thwarted by the weakness of the body, and to go, to do, to carry out the moment's impulse—all become arduous or impossible. We have had such misfortunes and will have them again, so how can we count on an eternity of health, on an endless readiness to participate in the race of desire? This limitation, this liability to disease, should, if well contemplated, cut back our vanity and our fascination with trifles and make us realize the evanescence of these conscious hours. How long shall our breath flow untroubled, and to what honorable purpose should we set our strength? And when illness descends, voiding all plans, what wisdom will defend us? Reflecting daily, more than daily, on this common fate of mortal creatures, we will be moved to do our rightful work.

The third reflection taught by the Buddha we have already met—not, indeed, on our own initiative but by our unplanned presence at this funeral procession. We are sure to die. This is so true it scarcely bears mentioning, it seems. But it is also true that through the momentum of desire and action we find ourselves always assuming, taking for granted, another gracious stretch of days to wander through—year upon forgiving year in which we may leisurely revise our philosophies, start or close agreeable projects, and maybe settle someday into some kind of religious faith. Unmindful of death, we grow negligent and live like the froth on a splashing stream—disoriented, weightless, and without conviction.

When, however, we reflect on death mindfully—with equanimity and detachment, not nervous aversion—when we keenly remember the omnipresence of *dukkha*, we are brought into salutary contact with what is real; we learn the precariousness and the value of our thinking, vital moments. If there is to be any ascent to spiritual vision, any escape from careless habit, it must be now; it must be launched and sustained by our own determination. When the boundaries of human life are clearly seen, the beauty of the Dhamma shines all the more, inspiring us to use it for our safety.

The fourth reflection, after old age, illness, and death, is another profound, somber truth: all that is dear to us will change, disappear, depart; and we will be separated from all of it. Change occurs sometimes by catastrophic jolts and sometimes by scarcely noticed, crumbling degrees, with familiar things and people slipping away, receding gradually but unstoppably. We adjust, we adapt, but from time to time a pang of grief hits as we realize how much of the past good has gone, how helplessly we lose what we love and wish to keep. We struggle against unruly fate to build some kind of safety among family and close friends; but we never seem to make it whole; and grievously it goes on deteriorating here and there. A friend leaves town; a beloved relative dies; children depart for schools and adventures we have no part in.

Again, it is not the *possibility* of separation that we should reflect upon, but the certainty. No passionate clinging, no ingenious skill holds together that which by its nature must fly apart. Our friends and relatives, our homes and belongings, the places and pastimes we treasure—they all whirl near us a little while then slip away, losing their familiar outlines as they go. That is their nature. All formations, the Buddha taught, are impermanent. We are frightened when we detect the disintegration of the joys by which we have withstood sorrows; but we know no better recourse than to hold on as long as we can, lament at separation, and turn desperately to new seeming joys, forgetting as we can. Then we find ourselves back where we were before, besieged again and dreading the loss of what remains to us. Once more we fear to face, to oppose, the deep *dukkha* that swells through all conditioned existence.

But if in our sunny leisure the thought of loss makes us sad, what will the reality do? Would it not be wise to take the counsel of the Buddha and reflect, calmly and repeatedly, on the universal fact that things must change and drift beyond our reach? When we are prepared for loss, no longer supposing ourselves uniquely immune to natural events, we will have less shock, less pain to deal with, and vanity over possessions and pleasures will not obsess us.

By the first four of the five reflections we slow the charge of egotism and begin to break apart the illusions which imprison us. To know the limitations of mortal beings is to prepare ourselves for sensible action. With fantasies in abeyance, with nature blowing freshly through our minds, we are ready to do something about suffering. The fifth reflection taught by the Buddha is that we are the owners and heirs of our actions, and whatever good or evil we do will be our inheritance, will direct our fortune, will make up our future. Whether we know it or not, all of these countless intentional actions by way of body, speech, and mind will color the stream of our being, leading on naturally to harm or benefit. When we explore this fact we learn both our own responsibility and our own power to better our condition.

First of all, in considering the force of intentional actions we begin to realize that it is not just the general imperfection of nature that makes us suffer. All of us are subject to old age, illness, and death because we are caught up in this *saṃsāra*, this flood of conditioned existence; but we are not only passive recipients of misfortune. Through our own willed deeds we bring upon ourselves innumerable needless sufferings and, indeed, continually swell the flood.

But there is a second, bright aspect to this succession of causes. Every day we intend and we act, thereby impressing changes on the world, changes on our own lives. If, then, we can distinguish good from evil, and act upon the good, we will assuredly receive good results. There is no magic here, only nature playing out according to conditions. The careful, rational follower of the Buddha learns what causes lead to what results and then through his or her own considered actions sets up the causes for blessings. Abstaining from evil and cultivating the good, then, are not just abstract exercises in virtue but practical measures that work for our own well-being.

When the Buddha asks us to apply our minds to some reflection, or to cultivate one quality and abandon another, we may be sure it is always for the purpose of overcoming suffering. Contemplation of the truths of existence is difficult—our minds, long used to dodging, resist the discipline—but seeing how the world functions is the necessary preparation for transcending the world. It humbles us, but it informs and inspires us as well.

Another fine thing develops when these reflections are rightly carried out. This is sympathy, for when we calmly contemplate death approaching, when we see old age and disease impending, when we reflect on past separations and those to come, when we ponder our actions as seeds for the future flung into the wind, we are made aware, as we gaze around in wider and wider regions, that all mortal beings live thus, too. Their frailties seem familiar; their grief calls up our sympathy; and we recognize in them the same strife we thought unique to us. Such is the universal, mortal plight—to be harried by *dukkha* born of craving; and such is the way to transcend it—to live according to Dhamma.

When the Buddha asks us to reflect frequently on somber truths it is not to make us gloomy but rather to relieve us of shadows, to let us see our situation clearly, and to inspire us to the kind of action that will cheer us and lift us out of peril. With these reflections in mind, when we look around at the world outside our private concerns we see those concerns reflected back in a thousand forms. It may be that we are hesitant, fickle, and reluctant to confront our bad habits; but seeing fellow beings everywhere enduring *dukkha*, dealing nobly or badly with their fates, we must realize that we are not unique or alone in our uncertainty. These problems are universal and are magnified or diminished by the action, the free power, of each person. Action makes things as they are for each of us, and action purified in aim always will produce blessings.

What kind of action, then, are we doing this afternoon? Certainly we have our duties to carry out—mundane errands of no intrinsic grandeur, no manifest spiritual merit. But all meritorious action is founded upon the mind, upon the intention to behave nobly. To keep that intention alive and productive we must apply mindfulness to what is happening, observing what is advantageous or harmful in the streaming moments we live. If we understand the character of these moments we will not, under the enchantment of the sensory panorama, succumb to greed or hatred or foggy delusion. What is right before us now? Small errands and chores. Let us then carry our parcels with care; let us speak and walk with fair deliberation and watch for the signs that remind us of *saṃsāra*'s conditions. When we reflect on old age, illness, death, separation from what we love, and the inheritance we set up for ourselves by our deeds, we nourish the mind with knowledge of the real character of the universe; we are made more serious and more attentive to the potential of our daily actions; we are more prepared to restrain ourselves from error, to recognize what is wholesome, and to do such actions as help ourselves and others.

It is a fine day, all right, at least according to our taste and temperament, with the sun warming us agreeably through the still air. Above the street and the buildings there is a jumble of hills full of autumn colors and above that the blue, neutral sky. Now as we begin to listen again we hear, besides the passing cars, birds in the maples and the clatter of human work and the stray shouts and laughs. Though the weather pleases us we cannot relax and drowse, for the peacefulness in nature that we guess at is an illusion. Therefore let us go on through what is here to finish our errands, walk our necessary rounds, reflect with reverence on the laws of existence, and keep for our warmth and light not the declining sun but the ever-brilliant Dhamma.

The funeral procession has moved on through other neighborhoods, past other eyes, but in the currents of cars and pedestrians we still glimpse something of that ceaseless movement that is *saṃsāra*. When we have Dhamma to guide us, many processions—many sequences and series of nature—remind us of impermanence and our unfinished work. We remain subject to the sorrows of *saṃsāra* as long as our minds still harbor greed, hatred, and delusion, but as we work to overcome them, as we confront our factual condition here and now, we begin to lift ourselves toward the incomparable peace of emancipation. It may be that now we must brace ourselves to reflect on that which we would rather ignore, but in the doing, in the actual contemplation, we find not agitation but an expanding sense of tranquility. The earth grows firmer and the Dhamma lights up its contours and lights up our way to freedom. Here, on the sidewalk, in the fine yellow sunlight, is where we stand; and there, beyond all processions, beyond all grief, is where we might go.

11
By Means of Mindfulness

S ometimes in a day with events flying bewilderingly around us, or in a weary evening while we wait for the commotion within us to settle down, the feeling comes that we are missing or have missed something vital and significant in the ordinary, swift hours. Our perceptions seem to be sparks that give only the briefest light. We react fitfully, without much forethought, then later worry about our impulsiveness and our unsatisfactory memory which cannot quite bring back the moment's picture for a better look. Did we really see what was there? Did we behave in the right way? Agitated in the doing and confused in the remembering, we seldom prepare ourselves very well for the next important choice, the next danger, or the next glimpse of some beautiful truth.

If we wish to live a noble life and to make progress toward the end of suffering we must make sure, above all, that we are really aware of what is going on within us and around us moment by moment. Even if we are inspired by the ideals of virtue, concentration, and wisdom, and even if we are, theoretically, willing to act in the ways that the Buddha advises, still we must diligently observe the succession of causes and effects in order fully to understand our situation. It is not a question of getting more sensory experience. Sights and sounds pour in throughout our lives; sensations of all kinds pour in; but wisdom does not necessarily arise. Perception in itself is only perception—an impersonal mental function whose prodigious activity usually overwhelms us. Through poor attention we miss the patterns in the flood; we do not distinguish the useful from the useless. Certainly, then, we need a better means of making use of perceptions as they arise and pass away.

It is not that we have no power of observation at all, or that we cannot concentrate when we really must—but we are habitually inconsistent and hesitant in our efforts and are never sure, moreover, that we are observing the right things in the right way. Is it possible to hold off habit long enough to get a true picture of any event? And do we possess the kind of view that will help us to comprehend what we perceive?

The Buddha emphasizes the need for right view—a stance or belief according to reality and an understanding of what is wholesome and unwholesome. Happily, right view is obtainable by listening to the Buddha's teaching and then judiciously examining our individual experience. We should observe the process of perception systematically and patiently in order to learn directly something of the laws that drive this restless universe. We should notice, as objectively as possible, the moods and intentions that continually form within us. We should try to regard all things, internal and external, as not self. We should discipline ourselves in body, speech, and mind, so that the repercussions of our own deeds will not harm us. And beyond simply perceiving, registering phenomena in the primitive sense, we should be mindful—that is, we should try to note clearly, to make out patterns, to recognize distinctly the nature of perceptions and thoughts.

When an event is well comprehended as it occurs, reflected upon, and considered, we gain an immediate kind of knowledge that will be much more valuable than guesses made long after the fact. A swift, impartial comprehension of what is going on right now will have many practical benefits, since it is less often lack of strength or lack of will that frustrates us in our daily problems than misperception, confusion, and emotional agitation. When we possess good information about reality we are in a position to make good decisions. Our livelihood and our family duties will certainly go smoother if we make it a practice to contemplate—not merely glimpse—the many small instances of craving or compassion or other qualities that move us to act.

Yet there is more than this to be gained through developed observation. We should not forget what the Buddha never forgets—suffering and the ending of suffering. One important principle which even the newcomer to the Dhamma can easily appreciate is that there are within the ordinary mind certain tendencies which ought to be abandoned and other tendencies which ought to be developed, so that suffering may be reduced and removed. We cannot doubt that the evil and the good, or the unwholesome and the wholesome, when long nurtured and cultivated, will have their effects on us, though we may not be quite sure about the details of the process. If we have faith in the Buddha we will be inclined to accept his advice and follow at least the basic precepts of morality and make some attempt to improve our minds in the ways he recommends, but still more is required if we are ever to remove suffering entirely.

The Buddha explains what is good and bad, what should be followed and what should not; but our mere intellectual acquiescence will not help us much. Armed with the Buddha's explanations of reality, we must set about examining our own experience day to day so as to observe within ourselves the unwholesome and wholesome tendencies and then to deal with them sensibly. We need, moreover, to consider all the coming and going of phenomena through our senses in order to see, in more than a theoretical way, how causes run naturally into corresponding new forms, and how, consequently, the courses of action that we choose may carry us to sorrow or to tranquility.

Such personal, individual observation is necessary because only we have the power to correct our flaws and refine our actions. Those are not the functions of the Buddha or anyone else. We need such direct knowledge of reality as will motivate us to act rightly, and we get that by paying attention systematically to causes and effects. When we look upon the world in the right way, repeatedly and carefully, as the Buddha instructs us, we learn to distinguish perils and blessings—states of mind and actions to be abandoned and those to be cultivated.

In doing this work of examination we particularly make use of the seventh factor of the Noble Eightfold Path—right mindfulness. Even if we have had little knowledge of the Buddha's teaching, this factor should not appear strange to us at all; it is not esoteric and remote but plain and accessible (though by no means automatic). Mindfulness is alertness, attention, awareness of what is going on in the present moment. It is dispassionate observation, a quiet, consistent recognition of mental and physical events as they happen. It reveals the actual nature of the perceptions and feelings that rush through us all the time. It does not add anything to experience—it does not, as usual thinking does, imbue it with any desire or bias—but rather shows just what is actually present.

Right mindfulness is mindfulness or alertness which is directed to suitable objects, aimed at noble ends, well established, built up, and supported with virtue and concentration. The Buddha teaches four "foundations of mindfulness" *(satipaṭṭhāna):*

> *Here, bhikkhus, a bhikkhu abides contemplating the body as a body, ardent, fully aware, and mindful, having put away covetousness and dejection regarding the world. He abides contemplating feelings as feelings...mind as mind...mind-objects as mind-objects, ardent, fully aware, and mindful, having put away covetousness and dejection regarding the world.*
>
> (Majjhima Nikāya 10)

The practitioner sets aside the familiar covetousness and dejection— that is, he or she calmly withdraws from emotional attitudes toward the world so as to be able to observe keenly. What should be observed, then, are objects as objects, things considered dispassionately just as they are, not in relation to any self or ego.

The first foundation of mindfulness is just the physical body, this collection of material elements. Normally when we consider our own body we look on it with pride in its health and strength, or with anxiety about its weaknesses, or with fear, attachment, aversion, or some other emotional bias that actually prevents a true perception. But instead of thinking automatically, "my body," we should try to limit our contemplation to what our senses actually present, which is just evidence of a living body—a self which owns the body being only an extraneous idea superimposed on the immediate facts.

The body may be contemplated as an object of a particular exercise in meditation, by observing, for example, the coming and going of the breath, or the touch sensation of the abdomen rising and falling, or the phases of motion in the walking process, or the postures that the body assumes, or any of its other activities. The body can serve as an object of mindfulness at any time of day when we contemplate it, reflect upon it impersonally as a conditioned phenomenon which arises and eventually breaks up, and which is composed of impure, perishing parts—each part being only a temporary compound of impersonal natural elements. We can also practice contemplation of the body simply by trying to act, as the Buddha says, "in full awareness" as we carry out our daily routines; that is, not bumbling along in unconscious habit but taking care to notice the motions and sensations that occur when we walk and sit and eat and so on.

The second foundation of mindfulness, contemplation of feeling, does not refer to emotion but rather specifically to the pleasant feeling, unpleasant feeling, or neither-pleasant-nor-unpleasant feeling which accompanies a given moment of consciousness. When we perceive some object through any of our senses, when we become conscious of a particular sensory experience, feeling occurs—an agreeable or disagreeable or neutral sensation, depending on the nature of the perceived object. Such feeling when unwisely grasped may quickly provoke greed, aversion, or delusion, and thereby push us toward all sorts of trouble; but mindful contemplation of feeling prevents automatic grasping and gives us clear information about what is actually occurring.

Contemplation of mind, the third foundation of mindfulness, means the contemplation of the overall character of the mind at any moment; that is, clearly recognizing present mental states for what they are, knowing a mind affected by lust as a mind affected by lust, or knowing a mind affected by hate or by delusion exactly for what it is, without trying to pretend it is otherwise. Again, we should be dispassionately observing, noticing whether the mind is cramped or expanded, concentrated or unconcentrated—simply trying to obtain an accurate view of this mind without assuming that it *belongs* to us. In the Buddha's words, we should contemplate "mind as mind."

The fourth foundation of mindfulness is contemplation of mind-objects—the particular phenomena that bubble through the mind. These may be thoughts, ideas, moods, volitions, tendencies, and so on. They should be noticed as they arise and pass away—again, without grasping at them, claiming ownership of them, or identifying ourselves with them at all. When certain conditions appear (whether good or bad, internal or external, far or near) we should be aware of the fact, and when they disappear we should be aware of that, too. Mind-objects might be particular perceptions or aspects of Dhamma that we see arising within us or around us or that we consider intellectually. For example, we might reflect on the five aggregates that make up the person—material form, feeling, perception, mental formations, and consciousness—observing how they operate, how they come to be and change and cease and reoccur. Or we might note within us any of the five "hindrances"—sensual desire, ill will, lethargy and drowsiness, agitation and worry, and skeptical doubt. Or we might observe how the senses function—how sights, sounds, smells, tastes, touches, and mental phenomena continually affect the sense organs and produce particular states of consciousness. Or we might observe the activity of any wholesome or unwholesome factors when they occur in us, noticing how one factor tends to give rise to something else and hence how complicated states of misery or happiness are eventually built up.

In all cases, one who skillfully establishes mindfulness in any of these four categories of body, feeling, mind, and mind-objects "abides independent, not clinging to anything in the world." In order to perceive anything clearly we need some objectivity; so we should try, when perceiving any phenomenon, to regard it dispassionately, just as it is, without disguising it to make it more palatable. We may find such an effort difficult, perhaps partly out of lethargy and partly out of anxiety about what dangers may surround us. We would prefer, of course, to attend only to agreeable matters, and even a brief, impartial look at our own minds may suggest discomforting truths. So why, we might wonder, should we exert ourselves?

The Buddha assures us that this systematic practice of mindfulness leads to purification, to the overcoming of sorrow, and eventually to the realization of *Nibbāna*. This is because when an attentive person perceives things as they really exist then he or she discovers at last which way to go, what to develop, what to abandon, and how it is necessary to behave wisely for the increase of happiness. Certainly the Buddha explicitly instructs us in such things, and certainly we will be greatly edified by listening, but we also need the wonder and enthusiasm that come from discovering in our own experience the reality of those timeless, spoken truths. When we act according to doctrine, and thereby test and confirm that doctrine, we motivate ourselves—we gain the faith that even we, with our abundant weaknesses, can move by our own power along the Noble Eightfold Path.

Knowledge acquired in the cultivation of right mindfulness is knowledge to be used, not merely accumulated in the way we might casually stack up books in a corner of our house. Impartial observation of physical and mental phenomena, moreover, does not imply approval of them. We establish mindfulness on the four foundations in order to see clearly what is really going on within us and around us, so that we will know what we must do to improve our character. For example, if during the course of our contemplation mental states of anger, selfishness, or greed repeatedly arise, we should not assume that merely observing them is all that is ever required of us. Rather we should mindfully notice how it is that these unwholesome states come to be, how long they persist, and what seems to bring them to an end. Acknowledging the presence of defilements in the mind is necessary, but it is not sufficient for their destruction. We must go on, through all our hours, to use right effort to stop their growth and to get rid of them entirely.

We will admit in the abstract, no doubt, that greed, hatred, and delusion in their many forms are poisonous, but we need to examine ourselves with mindfulness in order to see exactly how we are harmed by them and how we must strive to abandon them. Informed action is called for. Remembering the Buddha's teaching on cause and effect, we should consider that afflictions will continue to arise and to persist as long as defilements remain in the mind—this is simply the way nature functions according to conditions—and no listless hope will forestall new afflictions. There must be a conscious effort to restrain and eliminate unwholesome factors.

At the same time, when we observe within ourselves the beginnings of *wholesome* factors—friendly thoughts, generous intentions, sentiments of good will, devotion to the Dhamma—we can reflect that these things, too, will have effects, so if they are developed, strengthened, and repeated we may expect an increase in blessings for ourselves and others. Right mindfulness will show the good that exists, and right action—virtuous action—will bring that good to maturity.

The correct practice of mindfulness is not, however, an automatic or easy thing. Energy and effort must be applied faithfully and patiently, because an untrained mind does not of its own accord settle upon an object and examine it thoroughly; rather it is accustomed to bumping around inconclusively, jumping here and there, and in the whim of the instant forgetting where it was and where it meant to go. We do not accomplish anything in the way of contemplation by letting the mind do just as it likes. Instead, progress depends on energetically disciplining the mind and putting it to work on particular objects. Good mental qualities must not simply be admired on the occasions when we happen to notice them occurring—like wildflowers that we have had no hand in tending. Rather they must be raised and protected by steady labor. Mindfulness will, like a light, make clear what is in shadow; but it cannot operate out of nothing, without support. There must be conscious exertion and there must be the force of concentration to bring mindfulness to brightness and full power.

When mindfulness shows up the world as it is we gain the information we need in order to act rightly for our own good. It is not that the landscapes we have to cross become miraculously smoother, or that our weaknesses disappear, but that we see better how to travel over the existing rocks. Mindfulness, moreover, reveals that the urgent object of our searching—our own welfare—is perfectly joined to the welfare of others, and that virtuous action promotes benefit all around. The Buddha says that if we wish to protect ourselves then the foundations of mindfulness should be practiced, and if we wish to protect others then the foundations of mindfulness should be practiced. "Protecting oneself, bhikkhus, one protects others; protecting others, one protects oneself" (*Saṃyutta Nikāya* 47:19). The doing of good requires, first of all, the perceiving of good, the mindful recognition of those courses of action which will lead to benefit. With an eye to our own welfare we decide to do this or that, and again it is by mindfulness that we can successfully carry out our purposes. But this effort for our own welfare works at the same time for the welfare of others—there is not opposition but rather perfect congruence. Our private work of mindfulness will make us more sensitive to living beings' sorrows and more capable of worthy action. And when with a generous wish we attempt to protect others, to give some happiness or relief from woe, we require and use more of this same right mindfulness, which will result in our own spiritual advancement.

Once again we observe the relationship between virtue and wisdom. By good moral behavior, guided explicitly by the precepts, we can achieve the peaceful conscience that favors the work of mindfulness; and with mindfulness we perceive again the necessity of virtue. To act effectively for anybody's benefit requires that we understand the landscape around us and behave according to noble standards.

When virtuous behavior is inspired and strengthened through the systematic practice of mindfulness, insight *(vipassanā)* into the fundamental workings of *saṃsāra* becomes attainable. In his recorded discourses the Buddha teaches at length about the principles that compose and organize the world; he supplies us with the essentials of right view, without which we will never find our way to perfect safety. Once we have learned where and how to explore we must go ahead and do it. Mindfulness should be directed not only internally—toward our own body, feelings, mind, and mind-objects—but externally as well, toward other living beings and all the world of objects. We need to learn that we are not unique, that the same facts of impermanence, unsatisfactoriness, and non-self are found throughout all of conditioned reality, that things appear and disappear by causes, and that only by astutely controlling our actions can we obtain lasting benefits.

Other lives, other places, other adventures may seem to us more fortunate than our own, more wonderful, or more secure; but when contemplated dispassionately they lose their shine of fantasy, and the same impersonal processes stand out. All that is constructed comes to dissolution. Intentional actions bring results according to their nature. Complete liberation comes about when defilements are removed from the mind.

Outside our personal preoccupations all scenes, when looked at with mindfulness, testify to the Dhamma. Everywhere we may see growth, age, death, and birth whirling on around us, heedless of anyone's approval or desire. Greeting an acquaintance after a long absence, we notice with dizzy wonder the changes in appearance and demeanor, and we begin to brood on our own changing form. We who observe, we who still await an indefinite fulfillment, are also changing in others' eyes. Noticing the flow of conditions all around, we must infer our own conditionality, our finiteness, and hence the need to act with wisdom and kindness in the fast-escaping moment.

When mindfulness is put to work in a systematic way we may call it meditation or contemplation. Daydreaming cut off from the facts of ordinary material existence slumps into vagueness, but sustained contemplation takes the moment, examines it with energy, seeks out the laws of reality within it, and uncovers meaning beneath the isolated phenomenon. Any sensation, however unique or interesting or disagreeable, arises out of causes, out of a pattern of conditions; and if we watch attentively we may see how these causes lead naturally to certain kinds of results, and how, perhaps, we might stop those causes or introduce others or behave in a systematic, reasonable way to avoid misery and gain benefit. Unhappy emotions, for example, that we mindfully observe within us may teach us not only about the unpleasantness of this or that specific reflection, but also about the untreated defilement of anger or selfishness that has brought us, over years, into such a jungle of sufferings. The single happy thought, too—the inspired, compassionate intention—arises from causes whose nature may be learned through contemplation. Observing the patterns of actions that lead to good, then, we should be moved to repeat and strengthen them.

Along with understanding of the underlying principles of joy and sorrow comes the beginning of peace. All phenomena will change. Those things that are not ours—should we not cease to grasp at them? Those things we can control—our own actions—should we not try to make them as beautiful and pure as we can?

When mindfulness is working, the inexorable sweep of seasons with their vast blooming and withering carries off our feeble pretenses. We see our deeds and the intentions behind them. By contemplating these and remembering the teachings of the Buddha we learn what virtuous acts we can do now to calm our up-and-down life and indeed to reach at last that deliverance wherein no fear or desperation is found.

12

A Defense
Against Pleasure

We are all aware of countless dangers that cluster around us through-out our lives, and we expend much worry and labor in guarding against physical, financial, and emotional harm. When, nevertheless, some kind of misfortune hits us, we usually try to bear it with some dignity, with as much fortitude as we can, for this, we have been taught, is the behavior of a mature person. We learn (to some degree, perhaps) to restrain our hopes judiciously, to regard troubles philosophically, and to stay cautious about hidden dangers which may yet strike us. Misfortune depresses us but at least makes us regard the world seriously; it provokes exploration and perhaps a reassessment of unwise habits.

Pleasure and good fortune, on the other hand, immediately inspire us to throw down all defenses and to dote on a world we formerly mis-trusted. When we get the chance to forget misery in the enjoyment of beauty and pleasure we almost never hold back but take in, as fast as our senses feed us, gargantuan quantities of sight, sound, taste, and more. Whether it be nature's flowers or the splendors of art or the comfort of fine houses, food, furnishings, and clothes, we open ourselves to them willingly, eager to possess, if only briefly, any sort of seeming goodness. We will stifle our tears and groans, perhaps, but not our exclamations of delight; in sorrow we will brace ourselves, but in triumph we will reel with merry negligence. Yesterday's fortitude yields to today's noncha-lance. Pain drives us—sometimes—to profound introspection and efforts of serious conviction; but pleasure—welcome pleasure floating sweetly through our senses—suggests a postponement of difficult matters: why *think*, now that happiness is here?

Such inconsistency normally does not bother us at all, as we notice only one aspect of suffering—the explicitly painful episodes. If we endure those with any self-control we think we have done our duty, and when the bad weather blows by we are ready to relax, leave our mental doors unlocked, and savor the sweetened atmosphere. Pain requires scrutiny, but pleasure we admit without question, with sanguine confidence.

But is caution only called for in the case of pain and dispensable in the case of pleasure? Why should there be such stark reversals in our conduct? Can we really assume that whatever comes accompanied by charm and laughter is necessarily benign? Perhaps we attribute a little too much innocence to nature. We will admit, no doubt, that suffering has its varieties and degrees, from terrible pain to the mildest irritation; and we will admit that pleasure also occurs in various forms and intensities; but we seldom doubt our perception that suffering and pleasure are utterly distinct, dissimilar things and that one is loathsome and the other absolutely desirable and worthwhile. What happens is that we confuse ordinary sensual pleasure with genuine happiness, which is a subtler state of spiritual well-being (more often imagined, perhaps, than experienced). We know when we are miserable, well enough, and we know when we are pleased or delighted, but we are not so aware of what exactly brings about these states or causes one to fade and the other to arise. Certain phenomena, when they contact our senses, feel pleasant, but whether they have any real benefit or harm is a subtler question that we seldom probe into very far.

Shall we then look a little further? The Buddha says that before he attained enlightenment he "went in search of enjoyment in the world," found it, and understood it well. He also went in search of misery in the world, found that, and understood it well. This might seem to cover the question sufficiently, but the Buddha was not content; he went on to search for and to discover escape from the world—that is to say, freedom from all greed, hatred, and delusion. Ordinarily we look at pleasure and pain as the two defining categories of our experience, supposing that we should strive to get as much pleasure and as little pain as possible. The Buddha, however, was seeking perfect happiness, the complete ending of suffering, and he did not see it in those constricting alternatives but rather in liberation from the whole maze of desire, aversion, and ignorance.

The enjoyment or gratification brought about by the pleasures of the senses is so distracting that it is easy to overlook the associated misery and also the possibility of a higher attainment. Therefore the Buddha describes to his followers both the gratification in pleasures and what it leads to when there is no careful attention.

> *And what, bhikkhus, is the gratification in the case of sensual pleasures? Bhikkhus, there are these five cords of sensual pleasure. What are the five? Forms cognizable by the eye that are wished for, desired, agreeable and likable, connected with sensual desire, and provocative of lust. Sounds cognizable by the ear…odors cognizable by the nose…flavors cognizable by the tongue…tangibles cognizable by the body…. Now the pleasure and joy that arise dependent on these five cords of sensual pleasure are the gratification in the case of sensual pleasures.*

> (Majjhima Nikāya 13)

Certain kinds of pleasure arise naturally from the activity of the senses, but for one who is ignorant and unrestrained there are serious dangers which follow upon the indulgence in those pleasures. If one does not understand the empty, ultimately unsatisfying nature of all sensual delight, one will be quick to grasp after more of the same. A bite of fine food, for example, will taste delicious, will provide a momentary gratification, but will not abolish the arisen desire. The taste is "provocative of lust," so if one does not reflect properly one will be spurred to follow after the vanished pleasure, to trouble oneself to renew it, to magnify it, if possible; and thereby one is drawn toward peril.

But how, we might wonder, can the mere fading of a taste sensation, or of a lovely phrase of music or any pleasure at all, produce any real suffering? We know these small joys are impermanent, but are there not always more of them to be found? Here we should remember that while pleasures are abundant (or rather *seem* abundant) they are not easily grasped, and in the reaching after them and the holding on to them there are many dangers. The pleasant taste, intently examined, is an evanescent, momentary thing which does not satisfy the mind that wishes to luxuriate in pleasure. There must be more tasting, more savoring; but this is not practicable because repetition ruins the uniqueness of the delicacy we crave—we can only eat so much of anything before we get sick of it and want something else. So either we fail to get the imagined pleasure—and that is unpleasant—or the little we get fades away—and that is unpleasant—or we get a lot and find it actually distasteful—and that too is unpleasant. This is not to say there is no pleasure in tastes or sounds or smells or other sensual objects— there is; the gratification certainly exists, but it is a volatile phantom that cannot be held. In all sensual matters, then, mindfulness and restraint are great virtues that prevent the suffering that otherwise occurs.

The Buddha points out that a man who desires sensual pleasures must find the means, the wealth with which to obtain them. This entails labor in some trade, accompanied by the natural sufferings of cold and heat, accidents and injuries, along with general struggle, pain, fatigue, and other miseries. If his efforts to get that wealth fail he cannot enjoy the pleasures he wants and is plagued with frustration and dissatisfaction. If he suc- ceeds in accumulating wealth then he must protect it, and he is seized with worry that he may lose it. Then (as all things are impermanent) it may be that he does eventually lose some or all of his gains and suffers still more. All this is part of the danger of sensual pleasures—not apparent at first, perhaps, but nonetheless real and worthy of examination.

Furthermore, the Buddha observes that people fired by the passion for sensual pleasures take to quarreling. The desire for wealth and the sensual gratifications of wealth cause even close relatives to argue, to compete, to fight. They attack one another with words and fists and weapons and as a consequence suffer pain or even death. This is appalling and deplorable—but not so rare as to surprise us much. Such is this world— raging with desire—and such is the danger in sensual pleasures.

Again, "with sensual pleasures as the cause, sensual pleasures as the source, sensual pleasures as the basis, the cause being simply sensual pleasures," peo- ple commit all kinds of immoral deeds—unwholesome *kamma*—which lead to misery and suffering in this present life or to rebirth in wretched circumstances in the future. Not understanding and not restraining their desires, they run, seeking pleasure, deeper into suffering—a frightful irony endlessly repeated throughout *samsāra.*

As so often in the teaching of the Buddha, we see here a succession of conditions: out of ignorance about the nature of reality one craves objects, pleasures, and powers. Pursuing these greedily, one becomes lost in delusion, conflicts with others, performs bad actions, and suffers the painful results of those actions in this life or a future life. Moreover, without virtue, concentration, and wisdom one may easily repeat the agonizing folly, endlessly staggering after the phantom of sensual delight.

Certainly none of us would wish to continue on a path that we knew for sure would bring us to disaster; but as we are naturally much inclined toward sensual enjoyment we may keep on anyway unless we get enough knowledge and persuasion to do otherwise. Thus the Buddha is careful to show us the dangers that will arise if we charge ahead heedlessly and advises us to be vigilant—not only toward those things that obviously threaten us, but also toward those which, if embraced unwisely, may blur our understanding and push us down the slope to misery.

It is not that these five "cords" of sensual desire—these pleasant forms, sounds, odors, flavors, and tangible sensations—are intrinsically evil; ultimately they are only empty formations, transient phenomena without substance. But to all confused, excitable, and uncertain beings they are dangerous and should be regarded with much caution. The Buddha compares sensual pleasures to a blazing grass torch carried against the wind: if one does not quickly drop such a torch one will suffer terribly. It is not that the torch desires to burn the person who holds it, but conditions are such that he or she will be burnt; thus it behooves any sensible person to avoid those conditions that naturally lead to harm.

The *arahant,* the perfected person, has abolished all sensual longing and is unattracted by sensual pleasures; but the ordinary person must always be on guard against the deceptive promises of the senses. Visible forms, sounds, smells, and other sensual objects may be very sweet, appealing, and gratifying, but their influence does not necessarily end with their enjoyment. The mind may be swayed; greed may be excited; delusion may begin to overwhelm judgment; and bad habits of behavior may take hold. We all like to think ourselves independent, critical observers of the world, but in truth we are susceptible to the charms of the senses and not as careful as we ought to be; so we need the help of the Dhamma to govern ourselves wisely.

It is obvious that the Buddha's warnings about the dangers of sensual pleasures go entirely against the custom of the world at large, which regards self-restraint as pointless and stifling and sees sensual pleasures as absolutely good, genuine, available, and unquestionably worth pursuing. Suffering, in the worldly view, is an unpleasant accident, an embarrassment best ignored or covered with entertainment, distraction, and happy passion. The fulfilled life is thought to be one of coarse magnitude— much wealth, many possessions, intense excitements, copious praise and attention—in short, the zealous accumulation of whatever seems attractive. Whether such accumulation ever actually turns out to be truly beneficial for anyone is uncertain, but the idea is to go racing through life with such avidity that there will always be some new taste imminent to distract us from any accidental sourness.

This is ultimately a sorrowful enterprise. Whether or not a person consciously intends harm to others in his quest for personal gratification, because he is impelled by craving and does not know what is worth obtaining, he may easily succumb to bad tendencies, neglect the good, and slip into wrongdoing:

> *Inflamed by lust.... Incensed by hatred.... Confused by delusion, overcome, his mind obsessed, one chooses for one's own affliction, for others' affliction, and for the affliction of both, and one experiences mental pain and dejection.*

> (Aṅguttara Nikāya 3:55)

In emphasizing the danger in sensual pleasures, then, the Buddha is not trying to prevent us from obtaining happiness but rather to keep us out of pain and dejection and show us the real path to happiness.

Ungoverned, heedless sensual desire obviously tends to produce suffering, but sensual desire need not be always gross and avaricious to cause harm. The pleasures sought may be of a higher quality, found in music and art, edifying travel, and the exercise and enjoyment of personal talents. These pleasures in themselves are not necessarily bad—they may be very refined—but they are still unreliable. The danger occurs for the grasping mind that does not realize the impermanence of what is grasped. Even a person of mild temperament and cultivated sensibility imperils himself if he is still looking only to what are, ultimately, sensual pleasures for his safety and well-being. Lovely sights, sounds, smells, flavors, and touch sensations may beautify the flying moment—they do not strengthen the mind; they do not lead to peace.

Whatever sensual delight we grasp at, whatever material thing we seize upon as an undeniable blessing, is by that grasping turned into a source of pain. All compounded, conditionally arisen things are inherently unstable and sure to change, while the human mind insists on permanence, or thinks it can cope with change if it comes. But the potential for suffering, as the Buddha gravely declares, exists in all objects:

> I do not see even a single kind of form, Ānanda, from the change and alteration of which there would not arise sorrow, lamentation, pain, dejection, and despair in one who lusts for it and takes delight in it.

> (Majjhima Nikāya 122)

We are always in search of some kind of pleasant feeling or sensation which will hold still under our fond gaze, which will delight us indefinitely; but all phenomena without exception change, disintegrate, shift into new forms, disappear. What then is our proper course in such a slippery world? What sort of freedom is possible here? The answer follows naturally and simply once we have comprehended the gratification and the danger of sensual pleasures:

> And what, bhikkhus, is the escape in the case of sensual pleasures? It is the removal of desire and lust, the abandonment of desire and lust for sensual pleasures. This is the escape in the case of sensual pleasures.

> (Majjhima Nikāya 13)

Normally we think of happiness as an acquisition, if not of gross material riches then of other sorts of blessings in the form of amusements and entertainments; and the idea of abandoning or restricting them seems preposterous. But surely, before all else, the establishment of happiness or contentment must require the removal of that which continually generates misery. There can be no long happiness, regardless of the gifts of fortune, while the old insatiable passion for sensual gratification still burns. If we cease to obey the thoughtless urge, however, if we step back from the stampede to enjoy, we will be free from a grueling bondage, free to live happily.

But how is this to be accomplished? First of all, we should note that the Buddha is not saying we should starve ourselves and despise all beauty. Nor is he saying that all gratifying sensations are entirely false and poisonous. Through his own experience he learned that pleasure does arise from such sensations but that it is simply not a substitute for the joy of spiritual purification. Along with sensual pleasure comes considerable danger, to which a wise person should pay heed. Understanding the unstable nature of the world and the impulsive nature of the human heart, the Buddha shows that there are degrees of happiness or contentment and that the wise will forsake what is low and coarse in order to reach what is pure. It is a question of gradual education, gradual perception of what is really to our advantage to pursue.

Freedom from the oppression of the passions comes from the discipline of the balanced, moderate "middle way," the Noble Eightfold Path, which does not turn either toward bitter asceticism and self-torment or toward gluttonous self-indulgence. The middle way prevents us from being carried away by our habitual wants and allows us to see for ourselves the gratification, the danger, and the escape regarding sensual pleasures.

The correctly practicing lay person, then, begins to train himself or herself by observing the five moral precepts carefully; that is, by abstaining from killing, stealing, sexual misconduct, lying, and intoxicants. This in itself averts much danger and brings much gladness, for excesses are thereby limited as a matter of course, and the mind is to that extent lightened. When heedless extravagances of pleasure are by one's own will ruled out, then one learns, perhaps with surprise, that a contemplative, energetic, and frugal life has its own joys, and that a lack of feverish entertainment is not the frightful impoverishment it seemed.

If the taint of sensual desire is to be removed from the suffering mind it must be seen exactly for what it is. This requires alertness, attention, mindfulness directed at both the attractive and the unattractive objects that appear through our senses. All phenomena, whether pleasant or not, are inherently temporary, so the craving for this or that is a craving for mere soap bubbles, a clutching after what is already, in effect, on the way out of existence. Through systematic mindfulness, undiverted by the superficial allure of objects, we can learn this momentous fact in more than an intellectual way and thereby invigorate our will to keep ourselves free from ignorant compulsions.

The fulfilled Buddhist life, though it requires work, is not some grim asceticism. The Buddha says that he sees living beings burning with sensual desire and he does not envy them, because he experiences a higher, finer pleasure that is not sensual and not harmful. This is the sublime pleasure and happiness found in the *jhānas*—meditative states of exalted peace and concentration—and in the "immaterial" states beyond those, and in the supramundane stages of holiness which culminate in *Nibbāna*, the ultimate liberation. Moreover, the Buddha says there is the happiness of sensual pleasures and the happiness of renunciation, and of the two the happiness of renunciation is the greater. The Buddha teaches the Dhamma, we should remember, for the elimination of suffering and for the "profit, welfare, and happiness" of living beings. The right course for followers of the Dhamma, then, is to strive to rise from painful sensual imprisonment to the relief of liberation.

As long as we do not see anything nobler than sensual gratification, and as long as we do not experience higher states, we will remain liable to sensual attractions—this is entirely natural. But this does not mean we must remain under the absolute control of sensual desire, forever sent running here and there in miserable subservience. We can, if we so determine, exert our will to abstain from unwholesome courses and to develop higher states. Protected by observance of the precepts and by faith in the Buddha, we can live honorably in the world as it is and make progress toward the ending of all suffering. Sights, sounds, smells, and the other sensory events come to us accompanied by pleasure, pain, or indifferent, neutral feeling. All these things are conditioned, impermanent, and unreliable; like the colors in the clouds at dawn or sunset they have no substance or endurance and do not merit our passionate attachment. If a thing is painful, it will change; if it is pleasurable or neutral, it will change as well. An experienced mind looks past all these for satisfaction.

As children we were fascinated by colorful and noisy things and leaped without restraint from one to another; but as we grew older we began to look for and to appreciate stronger, sounder qualities of goodness, worth, and purity. As adults, then, coming to realize that all enchantments and fascinations of the senses fail and vanish, we should, inspired by the teaching of the Buddha, seek knowledge, seek goodness, seek liberation. Through such understanding and striving the full maturity of the mind can be found.

13
A Pilgrimage in Autumn

Out in the country in late autumn, late in a gray afternoon, we are walking, striding, still with a certain determination, along a path that will bring us back into the circle of society again. It has been a long hike already, one of those jaunts on which we have hoped to relieve our worries through exercise and silence. We know the way, or think we do, having casually planned out a loop through this region of park land, and it should not be too far now back to the highway and the troubled sphere we live in. The wind is cold, but we are dressed warmly enough so we do not suffer too much at the moment from physical causes.

We would have wished for better weather and perhaps for better scenery. As it is, we have let the weeks blow away until the spectacular changes of autumn are all but finished and even the trees with some color left look ragged and weary. Cold woods stretch out on either side. We did not think this land was really so remote, but we have met no other walkers and the solitude seems strange and interesting now. The land slopes and swells gradually, without drama. When we reach the crest of a wide, bare hill, hoping for a glorious view of autumn distances, we find that the world sinks far away on all sides into uncertainty and mist—immense and mysterious and disconcertingly without the definition we would like, with even the stones and trees all around melting into vagueness. The sky as well shows no distinct shapes, merely rolling and blowing in gray indifference.

Out here in the country the world looks different—not necessarily more beautiful or cheerful, but more dignified, at least, more graceful and significant. We had been intending to enjoy some of that autumn beauty, but if we cannot we may as well take meaning instead—or not even meaning if we think of it as chunks of information or succinct conclusions, but perhaps the intuition of splendor that the land inspires in us. For we feel that the land is old, ancient with respect to us and our ancestors. Empty woods all around, windy solitude, antiquity, huge oaks in the distance—these shrink us almost to nothing, yet impart something of richness and freedom. We hurry on through our trivial moment with the intention (frail as it is) of glimpsing certainty in old things, great things not made by man.

The noise, speed, and brilliance of what is called society do not, it seems, satisfactorily answer our longing for certainty; at any rate, from the stimulation of our social life we have turned aside for a while, to get far enough away even from ourselves so that we might look around unimpeded and contemplate whatever is noble and true. Out here we walk through the wind that streams and lags and streams again, exploring the cold, vital, primitive land until we feel somewhat less bound to our old preoccupations, more concerned with wind, creeks, and brambly meadows. A day of sunshine and stillness would have given us more pleasure, but by now we are not really sorry about it, for the gray weather smoothes a fine wonder over everything, suggesting greater truths than we might have suspected in more conventional beauty.

While we are lost in the profundity of the season, the work of walking and looking around becomes agreeable. With no particular excitement we observe the doves flying over the woods and the yellow leaves coasting down from maples to our path. It is not exactly that we forget our problems, but they take on something of the nature of the doves and the blown leaves—phenomena that sail across our consciousness without violence, just parts of the endless, amazing flux of things.

Exercising the body, attending to the senses, watching perceptions pouring like the wind, we begin to suspect that this "I" we have been so concerned with could be neglected with no loss in tranquility. Surely, just to walk, just to observe the blowing pieces of the world, requires no self, no self-regard. Such a distance we have come today, and the path seems quite oblivious, the sky quite untouched by our presence. Whether we despair or exult, the greater universe tumbles on all the same and blessings and troubles come and go; so why should we waste our thought in momentary conceits? The late autumn around us gigantically blows away into winter, and it seems possible we might find peace in the very impersonality of that—seeing and hearing and smelling with no special claim on what streams in and streams away.

We are glad to notice that we are partly relieved of care as we walk like this far across the alien, vacant land. Somehow the remote grandeur here sets us free to contemplate without expecting any charm or profit; and in our lack of expectation even bare saplings and yellow grass seem welcome and interesting. Stalks of dead weeds sway stiffly in the cold wind, and they too in their plainness and austerity give us some taste of a curious emptiness. For a while a muddy rill runs alongside the path, but it too is so far outside our usual notions of beauty that we waste no time in trying to imagine it as lovely. It merely trickles and flows according to conditions—and that perception somehow suffices us for now. It seems the more attentive we become to the changing world the less our personal troubles oppress us.

— We are wandering, it might be, through a boundless country of inexhaustible promise, full of themes for reflection, until it seems that if we walked long enough, if our breath did not give out, we might arrive at last in the certainty we have so long desired. But after a while our breath is not so strong, and our legs are getting a little tired. We stride through the cold weight of wind with less vigor, smiling ruefully at our forgetfulness; for it is surely not the walking, not the physical going, that will ever liberate us from our woes, but the conscious abandoning of clinging. It is right to be attentive, but we cannot think that a passive browsing through sensations—no matter how refined—will ever end in certainty and peace. Causes pile one upon another—like the leaves that stick and pile in the weeds—and produce results whether or not we understand the process. As long as ignorance is left free to work, as long as craving goes unrestrained, we cannot expect to escape from the grip of suffering. The real beauty and profit of this afternoon's hike, then, may not be in the welcome colors or the exhilarating mystery of the landscape, but in a deeper mood they suggest to the mind—the attitude of watchfulness, the respect for universal principles, the awareness of change. How we contemplate the impressions on our senses and how we discipline our daily actions will determine how far, in the noblest sense, we will travel.

Back in the world of warm rooms and social laughter, we had (we thought) a certain presence. Within those comfortable limits of walls and ceilings we considered ourselves significant and solid (if not as contented as we would like to be), and the hubbub and the crowded humanness there reassured us or at least kept up an illusion of purpose and busy self-hood. But out here the proportions of space overwhelm us, and we are reduced to a timid, tiny creature in the vast, cooling season. Although we stare left and right far off through the stark woods our gaze never comes up against a house, a car, a human being, or any symbol of a tame and managed life. We keep looking to be sure, amazed and mystified, until it becomes possible to imagine that the alien, primitive landscape simply has no limits at all. The narrow path ahead of us winds down into the next valley and up through vines and bushes and on again out of sight without sign of ending. It is hardly more than a deer track, but it seems it will outlast our human strength. How quickly our vanity is routed by the empty land. We go on in silence, marveling at the scenes that continually take shape and dissolve again.

Will it rain? The clouds seem thick enough. We should be coming back to our starting point soon, but it may be that we have detoured too carelessly and left ourselves with a long returning hike—if indeed we have not crossed the border into some primeval infinity. Rain would be a nuisance; rain would be a misery. Now we are getting a little cold, and we must acknowledge a certain fear of this empty country we meant to enjoy. Here no room echoes pleasantly with our voice. No sounds or signs confirm our importance. We wander now beneath a grove of huge oaks, looking far up with childish awe at the great crooked limbs shifting in the wind and the remaining leaves shaking wildly.

Often we have intended to seek out truth, to get a true picture of our own condition, but out here in the inhospitable land as the season runs by overhead the only truth that seems near is a profoundly perplexing one. With our connections to the babbling world severed, with mind and body roaming along an unknown path, we suspect an emptiness within as well as without. With no one to nod back at us, to encourage our sense of ego, we can only hurry along dazedly as thoughts and moods float loose. We have asked rhetorically for truth but perhaps all along we have really asked for the world to declare itself in our favor, happily revealing itself to be just as solid and benign as we have wished. And now as we see ourselves inching across a windy immensity we cannot hope for that at all but must confront the possibility that we are another conditioned pattern of events in the endless weaving of nature.

To perceive this is not a bad thing, as it turns out. Already we have noticed the exhilaration just in observing and letting the world fly by; and to let our own thoughts go the same way as the detached leaves might be no more troubling—might even be a relief, if we could achieve it over our fear. It is only the defilements of mind—greed, hatred, delusion, and their baleful offspring—which flourish in the obsession with vanity. A peaceful mind is surely a mind unburdened, relieved of the exhausting weight of ignorance. Out of ignorance we crave and cling—this is our ancient habit—but if in an attentive moment we sense some breeze of a selfless truth should we not make sure to learn the bracing lesson?

The ground on both sides of the path now is deep with still-unfaded red and yellow leaves. Off in the distance we see many old stumps and boulders that stand out like dignified monuments for past worlds, but over their cold shapes, too, brilliant leaves blow and settle. Everywhere the somber, silent earth is covered with color. Next week, after a fading rain or two, who can say? But should we complain, should we lament imper-manence? The main spectacle of autumn has already finished, and we have survived well enough. If we are taught the possibility of freedom by such a gray afternoon as this, perhaps it is not the beauty after all that mat-ters most but the looking into the laws of things, which may be done in any season. If the rain and snow soon destroy these colors there will be others to come, and other days and weathers to declare the same truths.

When our human vanity is jolted by the heedlessness of nature we are usually driven back toward the reassurance of society; but if we can restrain ourselves a little, if we can contemplate these facts of change and emptiness, we are enriched and enlivened. To have been born in this star-tling human world—what fortune! And to search for liberation—what blessing! We discover our frailties but we discover too that it is possible to breathe and walk and watch the world from more than one selfish, artificial point. Long used to habit, we become unexpectedly elated when habit will no longer serve and we are forced by the lonely, beautiful country to teach ourselves from the stuff around us. And it is not, we now discover, just a matter of choosing paths back to parking lots, but of questioning our purposes and duties as conscious beings. With the wind pouring timelessly, what of our human spark? What warmth might we foster, what greater light might we attain?

On a day when most creatures are crouched in their burrows we are out to forage for meaning, though no physical need compels us and though we might easily entertain our minds with a dozen distractions. The sky and the forest certainly have not undertaken to teach us, but in their natural operations they let fall some fruits untouched by the squirrels and the birds—solitude and silence, clouded distances, the shock of cold wind, the scent of autumn's shriveled greenery, even the sudden loneliness we feel in leafless groves. By these things we are nourished. What began as a walk, as haphazard exercise, is now a pilgrimage to understanding, and the more we admit this to ourselves and ponder it the more the scenery seems to shine with significance. We cannot organize our intuition into words, or precisely picture the goal, but our mood is freer now, our steps seem to fall with greater deliberation, and we look around us with an unaccustomed readiness.

Now the path leads us through acres of thick pines where the wind shoves at soft green branches in a dimmer light; and again we are lost in a country without limits, winding through the rough, primitive trunks with amazed eyes. It is a world not cut down to our dimensions and a time not ruled off for our convenience, but strangely we now feel no gloom. We are even, despite our shivering, emboldened to voyage on toward hills and creeks and inspirations not yet known. It is not that we must have a lovelier landscape or that we expect some singular sign—some article of scenery in itself—to touch off a definitive insight; but the repetition and reinforcement everywhere of restless conditionality gradually raise the heart to an ever keener alertness.

We have been walking for our own good, and now it seems that the good may lie in the getting away from the illusion of self, in a loosened, unrestricted view of pinecones, clouds, and all formations that roll through our senses. The weight of each footstep, the stretching of muscles, and the gusting breath within us, considered objectively, show no more uniqueness than the needles on the path or the stray twigs that drop through the pines. Volitions, moods, and memories, too, slip through the moment with nothing to mark them as ours. Should we not heed the obvious? We stride long, we shake our feet free of vines; and with a like effort we might free our minds from the bonds of self-concern.

Now before we have quite adjusted to this place the whole pine forest with its scents and motions is gone (another mere phenomenon vanished) and we are sailing out in more open country with saplings and yellow grass rolling on and giving way in the distance to big oaks again. Does the land ever end? Does *saṃsāra* ever end? Still the stream of gray clouds issues from that horizon, but we cannot believe the goal of our pilgrimage is literally there or at any geographical spot yet to be found. The search for that which does not fade away crosses into a greater country of contemplation whose wide reaches are nevertheless no farther away than our faculties of sense. Sights, sounds, smells, tastes, touches, and mental phenomena flood the moment with evidence of change; and this change, this impermanence, cuts against the dream of self. When, we wonder, shall all delusions fall and the unfading goal be known?

We have noticed something of this impermanence all through our lives; but seldom, perhaps, have we looked into it with a conscious will. The Buddha says that the perception of impermanence should be developed in order to eradicate the "I am" conceit. In one who perceives impermanence the perception of the truth of nonself becomes established, and such a person attains the eradication of the "I am" conceit; and that, the Buddha says, is "*Nibbāna* here and now." Usually we have shuddered at impermanence and turned aside to ever louder distractions, but when, as now, we try to contemplate things with mindfulness as they arise and vanish, we find that fear, too, is a passing state, and all the uproar of conceit seems thin and futile. Then with a purer will, a steadier effort, and a more concentrated vision might we not hope to get beyond all delusion at last?

We sense an urgency in the wind and the clouds and the trees, an urgency of change, as nature without rest keeps on discarding its wildflowers and its snows and all its seasons. We are sorry enough that our gardens and our summer reveries are broken up by bleak autumn, but we should see that this autumn too, with its rains and frosts, is less a state of being than a stream of change, an unstayable movement into something else. Even winter is no conclusion: it too will not lie quiet long but must melt itself into yet another fever of greenery—and still the empty urgency is unappeased. But when we wondering creatures are fortified with the Dhamma we need not be agitated into passion. Instead we must contemplate the streaming-on of things as it happens, bear with such change as fortune brings us, and seek peace in non-grasping.

On and on before us the path runs through the empty park land, and although we are tired we can still travel at a fair speed among the obstacles of nature. This path still leads, we think, the way we need to go, so we keep on against the sweep of the wind, striding as well as we can and feeling through our senses the amazing changes of the world. Sometimes a shape of unusual beauty rises before us—a tree that still holds its bright red leaves or a picturesque boulder on a hillside—but in a moment it too is behind us, and a habitual, almost irresistible impulse turns our eyes to seek the next remarkable sight on the path. But should we not try to get free of this endless strain of regret and expectation? Must life be a series of disappointing enchantments? All phenomena, of whatever brilliance or promise, are still impermanent, so why should we be looking forever among them for the ever more impressive experience? These things flash by beyond our control; but this mind which yearns and trembles might be tamed. By attending to the path right here we get over the rocky hills and across the thorny lowlands, and in the working, in the necessary striding and mindfulness, we find cause and effect marvelously operating. There is action and there is result. If we understand this principle we can surely make progress.

When the mind is put to work observing the rise and fall of phenomena it has less chance to misbehave, to run after distractions, to sink into delusion. Watching the present moment with the determination to know it clearly, the mind may begin to detect the deep certainties of existence which before seemed only hypotheses. When the immemorial illusion of ego is not attended to—is left behind for a while in the vigorous contemplation of impermanence—the mind is relieved of a terrible affliction. In self-restraint there is the paradoxical, beautiful beginning of freedom. Then land and sky which do not reassure, do not entertain, and do not even notice the pretensions of self display to the mind bold and inspiring truths.

Wandering out in this seeming desolation today, we have lost some expectations of pleasure but gained a thrilling immediacy, a sense of the awesome flow of time, the depth of changing space, and the surge and crash of powerful conditions. Surely we have lived too narrowly within the limits of self-concern. The more we require of the universe the more barren it seems, but when we discipline ourselves to watch its actual operations the more fruitful it becomes. We begin to perceive how the patterns of worldly things flourish and fall by conditions. This knowledge is not academic but concrete—breathed in with the wind, distilled from the rain and the earth. We see that happiness and suffering and good and evil are all possible, and that if we direct our own actions intelligently we might bring about blessings.

There is movement within us and all around us—change, development, and dissolution according to the rising and falling of conditions—but this movement in itself is not progress for us. We may be surprised, even delighted, by the prodigious cascade of changes, hoping that it foretells some ultimate blossoming of our destiny; but why should the roiling universe ever arrange itself for our benefit? Real progress can be found only in our own consistent action, in the determined pursuit of a noble ideal amid the restlessness of *saṃsāra*. Alone on the cold dirt track in the late afternoon, we know we cannot slump down on some convenient log or rock and simply *wish* ourselves at home. Rather we strive; we walk deliberately; we keep our balance as well as we can. For our spiritual progress, then, we must surely do the same.

Around us there is the certainty of impermanence, of unsatisfactoriness or *dukkha*, and of impersonality. But we must seek the certainty beyond the colors of the collapsing autumn, beyond all cycles of beauty. We struggle in a thicket of distractions; we find the path; and then, as hope expands, we keep on traveling in the promising direction. The path that truly lifts us and leads to safety is not a literal trail through the grass; but by means of these things that are concrete and present to our senses we feel more definitely the direction of the Buddha's teaching. With all these natural powers resplendent around us, how shall we guess the limits of our strength? Why not stride straight and see? From this to that, from here to there, forceful conditions grow.

Now, as the grayness of the afternoon deepens, we pass through a screen of woods and emerge on an open field bounded in the distance by a road. There, suddenly, is the parking lot; there is the remembered entrance to the park and the tamer land beyond. We pause, expecting any moment to relax into a state of relief and comfort. But still the cold, epic sky is flowing over us so magnificently that we cannot really believe we have completed our adventure, and we look on these incidental fences and cars with no special excitement, seeing them for the moment, strangely, just as more leaves in the gale, about to fly up with the next shock of wind.

We need rest today, to be sure; and we have our duties, our temporal work to do with honor; so we are glad enough to have finished this one, limited circle. But from this distance and after this tour through the empty land we cannot regard the worldly commotion ahead of us with quite the same fascination as before. The path that runs straight now to the parking lot does not, it seems, really end there but slips off under unpredictable skies into yet more amazing landscapes of mind. Our weariness notwithstanding, we would be traveling on that higher path.

14

ON THE WAY TO THE HIGHEST

How many times, alone in thought, have we worried over our need not just for lovelier possessions or higher honors but for some spiritual relief far beyond them, some arrival at a beautiful peace? Perhaps we pause to look out a window when a maple tree's leaves are turning and pass swiftly from that one brilliant vision to the hope for a greater splendor. How shall we get there? Or we hear, while absorbed in our work indoors, a sudden, fresh gust of rain and wind outside. What yet unseen truth does it signal? What tremendous, wild reality surrounds us? While we remain caught up in all the mishaps, pleasures, and disappointments of our lives, while each day's particular gain or loss will move us, we still grope for the right way, the higher standpoint. In our clearest, most honest moments we long to experience for ourselves, to know by our own effort an absolute, undefiled purity that will not die away.

When we study the Dhamma we find a practical path whereby to realize our noblest intentions. Learning that all good or bad formations come about through built-up factors or conditions, we must admit the encouraging conclusion that progress toward greater understanding and peace is certainly possible; and if it is possible, why should we not make an effort to achieve it?

Progress in the Dhamma is a matter of patiently bringing together the necessary factors, of successively using the wholesome states that appear to step up higher and higher, all the way to full liberation. Progress or decline happens—as all things happen in this conditioned universe—by way of causes, and in the teachings of the Buddha we find many illustrations of conditioned processes, many explanations of how one thing provides the basis for something else, and that for yet another thing, in a natural sequence that goes on whether or not we understand it or give our approval. If the appropriate conditions for a certain state arise, then that state will arise. As mortal beings encircled by perils we are eager to comprehend those processes which affect our happiness; and as a teacher with knowledge and goodness the Buddha spent his life explaining what we should know and how we should act.

The goal of the Dhamma, to put it in a phrase, is to get rid of suffering. This goal is achieved when the necessary factors are complete, when the right steps have been taken, when all defiling conditions have been abolished. Having reached the goal himself, the Buddha knew what was required, and he knew also the weaknesses of ordinary human beings. Therefore those doctrines he declared, those standards he taught, those practices he recommended were those he knew to be both efficacious and possible. The Buddha taught the Dhamma in differing degrees of sophistication and intensity to the lay people and to the Sangha of monks and nuns, but the fundamentals were the same and remain practicable today according to everyone's worldly situation.

Even if we feel demoralized, unconfident, and incapable, we should consider that the law of causality goes on operating quite impersonally, irrespective of our attitudes. If we actually do some meritorious action, for example—if we apply some wholesome effort—that will certainly have its effect, whether or not we expect it or set our hearts on it. In itself it may be a small thing, quickly fading, but if we follow the Buddha's instructions we may enlarge the lovely results and use them to inspire us more than we would have believed before.

Once Venerable Ānanda asked the Buddha about the benefit and the advantage of good moral habits. That such habits were worthy and healthy he could have had no doubt, but perhaps he was wondering, to what particular good end might they lead?

The Buddha answers that the benefit and the advantage of good moral habits are "nonremorse." Asked then by Venerable Ānanda what is the benefit of nonremorse, the Buddha says, "gladness." Asked what is the benefit of gladness, he says, "rapture." Asked about rapture, he says its benefit is "tranquility." Questioned further, he says the benefit of tranquility is "happiness"; the benefit of happiness is "concentration"; the benefit of concentration is "realistic knowledge and vision"; the benefit of realistic knowledge and vision is "revulsion and dispassion." Finally he declares that the benefit of revulsion and dispassion is "the knowledge and vision of deliverance."

Clearly the Buddha is describing here not just the blessings of miscellaneous virtues but a definite progression of wholesome states which leads on to full emancipation. The morality, the consistently good behavior which he so often emphasizes, certainly has many good consequences in the development of a person's character and in pleasant relations with other people; but it is interesting that here the Buddha singles out nonremorse as its particular benefit and advantage. Why should what seems merely a lack of something be deemed noteworthy? Let us consider the mental effects of self-restraint, moral discipline, and honorable adherence to noble standards. When one is training oneself in this way, evil causes are removed. There is then no regret, no guilty apprehension or grief based on ignoble deeds. Not doing harm, not causing misery to living beings, one has no fear of bad consequences, no self-disgust, no regrets to struggle with. This is a perfectly natural result. Being conscious, moreover, of having done right, having strived to become a better person, one feels mental relief and lightness—a kind of freedom which is a positive blessing in itself.

Good moral habits, then, are causes or conditions which give rise to the pleasant state the Buddha calls nonremorse. This state of freedom from remorse has its own potent tendency; it too is a factor in the arising of other things, and in this sequence the Buddha next specifies gladness. When there are good moral habits and when the mind is relieved of guilt, fear, and remorse, the way is opened for the blossoming of gladness—the relaxation of the formerly agitated mind, the upsurge of confidence and good spirits. Too often we think of gladness as the product of sensual pleasures, but the Buddha would have us obtain it, and notice it, through the true method of removing unwholesome conditions and fostering wholesome conditions.

This gladness is by no means the end of the practice, only one step, one factor in the great progression. The benefit of gladness—the advantage to which it tends—is rapture, joy, an unworldly, nonsensual pleasure of a mind free from its ancient burden of worry and passion. But even such a glorious feeling as this is still a conditioned, temporary thing, and thus not the highest, not ultimately to be relied on. It is only a pleasant and refreshing state which has its own tendency, its own further benefit, namely tranquility. When one is well practiced in virtue, relieved of remorse, glad, and inspired with nonsensual rapture, one is likely to experience great tranquility in body and mind. This tranquility is a steadiness, a deep serenity, a state of gratifying balance and ease.

The benefit that follows tranquility is happiness—a settled, pervasive peace and spiritual well-being. But such happiness, although it is very refined, is still conditioned and thus not complete, not perfect. It does, however, provide a serene foundation for concentration—that power of gathering and intensifying attention and applying it to specific objects and to the whole process of phenomena arising and passing away according to conditions. The result of such concentration is realistic knowledge and vision—seeing and understanding things according to their actual nature. At this stage one is no longer simply experiencing finer and finer states of body and mind, but is directly comprehending reality without delusion.

Such unhindered understanding might seem to be the logical end of the sequence, but it is not. The factor of realistic knowledge and vision leads on further to revulsion and dispassion—a surprising state, when we first hear of it, if we have been assuming that the progression must always be toward greater pleasure and satisfaction in observed reality. Far from delighting, the one who reaches this state sees the inherent instability of *saṃsāra*, recognizes its three characteristics of impermanence, unsatisfactoriness, and nonself, and experiences revulsion; that is, the drawing back from beguilement and misperception, the abandoning of fantasy, delusion, and fascination for the objects of the world. Knowing all these unsubstantial things for what they are, one naturally becomes dispassionate—free from the compulsion to pursue, no longer driven to grasp, to cling.

Then what is left? One more benefit, the greatest of all, follows from this. It is the knowledge and vision of deliverance. Seeing the universe for what it is, one destroys ignorance. When ignorance is destroyed the miserable craving which depends on it is also destroyed. When craving is gone the fire is gone, and there is no more *dukkha*, no more suffering. The enlightened person sees this and realizes this and is fully liberated.

"Thus, Ānanda," the Buddha says, "good moral habits lead gradually to the highest" (*Aṅguttara Nikāya* 10:1). Through the patterns of cause and effect, through the inconceivable complexity of actions and results, the Buddha traces out a line of causality which begins with ordinary moral behavior—something not out of the reach of any thinking person—and ends with complete liberation itself. We see in this summary the Buddha's abiding concern with the way phenomena are linked—how one thing gives an impetus for the arising of another thing. Liberation from suffering is the natural result of the destruction of unwholesome conditions and the growth of wholesome conditions. One who understands the principle of causality here should realize then that the Buddha's instructions are aimed at encouraging his followers to adopt those standards and do those actions which naturally fulfill the necessary conditions for liberation. If followers understand the logic of causality they will be all the more zealous in their practice.

But we might wonder whether such gradual progress through wholesome states is automatic or whether it requires exceptional talent or strength or some other vital ability. How can we move from one stage to another? Because all events depend on changeable conditions we are certainly not guaranteed the attainment of liberation, or indeed any lesser attainment. Our progress always depends on the conscious efforts we make. Nevertheless, when those efforts are properly made, there is a definite tendency toward higher development. The Buddha says, "For one who is virtuous and endowed with virtue there is no need for an effort of will: 'May nonremorse arise in me.' It is natural, monks, for nonremorse to arise in a virtuous man." Likewise for one who experiences gladness, rapture, tranquility, and each of these good states in turn, there is no need to formulate a special wish to reach the next higher state. It is not a question of wishing or desiring but of actively developing the qualities which make for progress.

We also cannot suppose that if we just observe, let us say, the five moral precepts with minimal fidelity we will be assured of obtaining nonremorse and the whole sequence of higher states. Rather the Buddha is saying that mere resolutions and protestations are beside the point: it is the cultivation of good conditions themselves that is important. When indeed one has mature virtue it is natural for nonremorse to follow. In other words, when there is virtue or moral firmness in a person the foundation for nonremorse is established; and when there is nonremorse the foundation for gladness is established; and so on through these successive wholesome states, each being the benefit and advantage of the one before it. But still, at the very beginning and throughout the practice, no one is relieved of the responsibility of working to bring about higher states of mind. Many cooperative factors are necessary along the way, and they do not occur by accident. The practitioner must exert himself to obtain a particular benefit, and when that benefit is obtained, even partially and imperfectly, it will resound through his whole character, enabling him to work all the more diligently.

Concluding his summary, the Buddha says,

> *In that way, monks, these qualities are integrated with the other qualities; and in that way these qualities bring the other qualities to perfection, for going from the Here to the Beyond.*

> (Aṅguttara Nikāya 10:2)

Not only do the good qualities outlined here lead on progressively to higher states; they also reinforce each other. We should not suppose, for example, that good moral habits are necessary only once, only at the beginning, or that gladness is simply a momentary stage, or that realistic knowledge and vision can only be experienced in utter perfection. Rather, good moral habits so pacify and cheer the mind that one is inspired to examine the laws of reality. As one examines, one perceives more clearly the beauty and advantage of virtue and concentration and is inspired to make further effort. To the degree that one develops these various qualities, one experiences more fully their blessings, until they are at last so developed that they culminate in liberation—in the knowledge and vision of deliverance.

Thus, with the guidance of the Buddha, it is possible to make use of the principle of causality for going from the "Here" of ignorance and suffering to the "Beyond" of full deliverance. If we worry that we are too weak or distracted or unsure to think about that goal, we might well reflect that the Buddha perfectly understood human weakness and yet taught the Dhamma as he did, knowing that a sincere person practicing according to good principles would find reassurance and strength in his or her own experience. At the same time, we should remember that cause and effect are absolutely neutral in their operations; in *saṃsāra* there is no built-in bias in our favor. When we strive consistently according to Dhamma, aiming at worthy attainments, progress can be expected; but when we grow slack or, worse, entertain bad intentions and otherwise misbehave, then the current of causality will run just as vigorously toward decline and misery.

In the most general terms, when craving exists, *dukkha* or suffering arises; when there is no craving, *dukkha* does not arise. In itself the principle of causality is neither good nor evil; but it may bring us good or evil depending on the nature of our deeds. The Buddha explains what sorts of deeds we should do—what sorts of conditions we should establish—so that good and not evil will be the natural result. Factors build upon factors gradually, and in any particular moment we may not be able to see the swell of potential or the alteration in our own character; but the Buddha has directly understood the sequences that lead to happiness and to pain, and if we trust his guidance we can work patiently in the present moment, knowing that the correct step now will bring us to the next correct step in the future.

In urging his listeners actually to practice the Dhamma, the Buddha sometimes gives a "progressive instruction"—one which does not assume any prior faith and which leads the listener on from the elementary to the profound in a gradual, comprehensible sequence. He first speaks of giving *(dāna)*—a basic practice which everyone can develop—because giving is in itself a wholesome action which brings happy results, and because giving has the salutary mental effect of weakening stinginess and the underlying preoccupation with self. Giving gifts or doing services for others, even when undertaken with difficulty or reluctance, naturally affects the mind in such a way that one becomes more and more inclined to further worthy actions and higher thoughts. This inclination is not a matter of intellectual resolve but rather of the sheer power of good action; one gives and one naturally feels inspired—that is all.

The Buddha then speaks of virtue—the moral precepts, principles, and standards which should be respected by anyone who wishes well for himself and others. Then he speaks of the heavenly worlds—those happy planes of existence where virtuous beings are reborn as a result of their good *kamma*. This present life will have its successor, and when virtue is faithfully exercised here, there will be tangible blessings in the future for the virtuous person.

With this foundation of hope and good cheer, the Buddha goes on to talk of the "danger, degradation, and defilement" in sensual pleasures, which, in spite of their immediate attractiveness, lead the careless person on to negligence, bad behavior, and overall decline. In contrast to sensual lust the Buddha raises the ideal of renunciation *(nekkhamma),* which the listener, if he has followed along so far, may now be prepared to appreciate. In addition to avoiding gross immorality, the faithful practitioner of Dhamma moderates and simplifies his life, no longer feverishly grasping after magnificent possessions or running after superfluous recreations. Renunciation, in the teaching of the Buddha, is not some painful self-torment but a blessing, a relief, a healthy removal of oppressive burdens. To renounce wisely is to step back from extravagance, complication, and passion and to seek contentment in simplicity and dignity. The commotion of the world is indeed thrilling, but as one draws back, and the cacophony fades and drops in the distance, the finer, lovelier tones of quietness can be heard.

At this point in the Buddha's gradual explanation, when he sees that his listener's mind is "ready, receptive, free from hindrances, elated, and confident" he goes on to reveal the Four Noble Truths: the truth of suffering, the truth of the origin of suffering, the truth of the cessation of suffering, and the truth of the way leading to the cessation of suffering. Here the Buddha explains the core of the Dhamma in its splendor and beauty; and whoever has followed him this far is shown how the Dhamma works to abolish the perennial problem of suffering, and how it should be practiced for the realization of happiness and the attainment of *Nibbāna.* This is exactly the intention, the function, the gift of a *Tathāgata,* for he is "one who shows the way." What happens next is the choice of the listener. If, out of his own faith and will, he does one virtuous act, and then another, cause and effect will build and move. Gradually one good thing leads on to higher things.

Throughout the discourses of the Buddha we again and again find this principle of causality taught and exemplified. Things come about gradually, progressively, as the necessary conditions arise. Liberating understanding, too, comes about through a gradual process as one brings together and fortifies the necessary good qualities. The Buddha says that in this doctrine and discipline there is "gradual training, gradual practice, and gradual progress." He teaches his followers gradually, urging them to accomplish one task and then another. Therefore we should not worry if, when we take up the practice of the Dhamma, all our problems do not at once dissolve or if we still feel much weariness and difficulty.

When we plant a vegetable seedling in our garden in the springtime we do not expect to be enjoying the produce in a day or two; we understand that work must be attended to, that conditions must be supplied, so that the plant will mature gradually according to nature and produce its fruit. The seedling, considered in itself, looks insignificant—it does not at all resemble the delicious fruit to come—but we know enough of this particular string of causality to be confident of a reward if we tend it properly. Likewise maturity of mind is not hurried by impatient desire but occurs only when mental cultivation has been rightly carried out.

When we set a seedling in the earth and tend it closely we participate in and adapt ourselves to the flow of causes. We add new conditions, and cause and effect take hold and grow. Never can we abolish the truths of causality, and never shall we turn the thistle into the apple, but by deeds in accordance with Dhamma we may see that what grows in our own mind's ground will be fair and sweet and free.

15
Belongings

After the death of a member of our family, after the funeral, the receiving of condolences, the adjusting to absence, the getting on with our routine, there come the long months in which we must decide what to do with the miscellaneous belongings of the deceased. The will has named the heirs of the bulk of the estate, but there remains, stacked in our attic or piled here and there throughout our house, an assortment of minor things that must eventually be picked over and disposed of. On this silent, bright winter afternoon we are not going anywhere and for the moment we do not feel greatly pressed by other duties, so shall we take a look through those old papers and knickknacks? Shall we distribute the residue of the past somehow into the present?

Brilliant sunlight falls on us as we carry bags and boxes past the windows and settle down for the chore. It seems a little strange to see these old possessions, remembered from another place or long stored away, now spread out on a table and arranged around us on the rug in the incongruous modernity of our house. To go through these will probably be a little depressing, but it must be done, and after all these months our grief is surely worn down enough to get on with the task.

What our elderly relative kept was what we all keep—mementos, letters, ancient bills and receipts, books, photographs, ornaments, diplomas, family records, programs for forgotten shows and ceremonies, odds and ends of clothing, medicine bottles, framed pictures, and many other dusty small possessions. Some of this is already packed in boxes, some merely swept up by us when we closed down the old house. We dig into it briskly, seeing much trash that can simply be discarded—envelopes, calendars, torn notebooks, business papers now devoid of significance. We drop these into the wastebasket quickly at first, determined to get through the clutter; but soon we slow down, reflecting that a certain care is warranted, as we are, in effect, editing history for future generations. Besides, we find ourselves wondering over trinkets, reading the dim handwriting on tattered notes, scrutinizing gray photographs for recognizable faces. We are modern, we are businesslike, we speed through a sleek and casual world; but still we have not quite adapted; and the fragile papers that crack in our fingers raise ghosts and regrets for worlds gone by. We are just curious, we tell ourselves, just interested in family history—and who knows what colorful facts we might come upon?

But even in the unsentimental winter daylight, time gets away from us. We read, we remember, we drift into reveries on the strength of faded papers. Lifting out one photograph, we reminisce over the likeness of a face we shall not see again; and then we find a newspaper clipping about a business function that took place before we were born; and beneath that lies a letter from our grandfather telling of times and people we do not know; and beneath that there is more—the jumbled signs and relics of vanished lives. These relatives preceded us, lived through their own turbulence, made of their time what they might, and left (probably with no particular thought of the future) these mementos which now seem to carry something of the gravity of history. Here in another photograph is our great-aunt—a young woman dressed in the fashion of the time, laughing with friends at a party. That was a world, that was a moment that flashed like light on a dashing stream; and we in our own moment, in the splash and brilliance of the present, gaze on with growing awe, unable to comprehend that such vitality could have been and could have vanished.

We should not, of course, be surprised at impermanence, for in our mundane routines we see an endless vibration of novelty—modern life being a mad discarding of one day after another. But still we have assumed that our existence, our self with its needs and interests, somehow rides on intact through the chaos. How long, really, can we believe in our spectacular uniqueness, as if we of all mortal creatures could survive the storms of time unaltered? Would we protest that we cannot notice the great currents that buffet us or that we are too delicate to confront a glaring truth? No, surely not—we would be ashamed, because doubts have shadowed us often enough, because we have glimpsed, in the lonely flight of traffic in winter darkness or in our own photographs from the past, the sorrow still showing through all distractions.

That fashions should change seems entirely right; that a world should disappear with all its vividness disturbs us. These pictures, letters, and trinkets tell us that our relatives, our ancestors, lived in a world of love and business and grief as we do, lived in their own makeshift permanence and perhaps thought it real, perhaps not. They are gone, in either case, and have left these signs that warn us—if we are willing to be warned— that whatever human strength can do must be done in a few bright, unpredictable years.

We would certainly wish to find within these bags and boxes some evidence of lives that were good on the whole, happily finished, and unregretted. That might relieve us of a little of the sadness we feel over the dissolution of those worlds. But what we find here are mostly mundane details of family, duty, recreation, and work—no statements of philosophy, no revelations of inner joy or despair. That far-away cousin, never known to us, and that ancient uncle, remembered only faintly from childhood, occupied themselves with the demands of the present, their present, and how far they imagined or pondered the future we cannot know, and whether they considered their lives satisfactory we cannot know. Surely they had their sorrows—their bereavements, sickness, failures, loneliness, personal and social disappointments of all kinds—and surely they had their gladness and laughter as well; but how did they balance out, or is there any balancing at all? We have not come to any trustworthy conclusion in our own lives, for *dukkha* is not banished by delight—they exist together in baffling contrast, in subtle or explicit strain. That is why, it may be, we look with hope toward others' lives. Did they, in their words and actions, accomplish what we have not accomplished? Might their examples suggest a course for us?

We read fragmentary stories out of these boxes of sentimental treasures; we imagine the adventures of our ancestors; we willingly forsake, for a little while, the whirlpool of self-concern to explore the mysteries of these belongings. Enigmatic souvenirs of distant places are mixed with

household odds and ends, yielding traces of history, clues to vanished personalities. It is not, we realize now, just curiosity that moves us through
these stories, but an ardent wish to track down some bright certainty
behind the forests of ordinary living.

Here, neatly wrapped, are carved wooden bookends in beautiful condition. And here is a woman's scarf, clean and folded—worn in youth,
perhaps, and poignantly outlasting that youth. We must pass these on to
someone who can use them. But whatever there was of wisdom or goodness in the owner, that we cannot pass on easily; that was at most an influence only, felt by those nearest, who might by their own efforts someday
arrive at a like beauty of character. From our ancestors we inherit material things—objects of worldly value or unworldly sentiment—while from
our own actions, far more certainly, we inherit joy and misery. These
belong to us when all else vanishes. Things can be used; they may remind
or move to meditation, but each of us in our transient worlds must act,
must work to gather the constituents of virtue.

Here is a heavy box full of old books—on accounting, engineering,
business, and other sober topics. But among them we find a few volumes
that make us smile—collections of poetry and children's stories, most in
terrible condition, some that we remember from our own childhood.
Were we the heedless children who wrecked these volumes, now come
back into our gentler hands? Were these intended to be passed on to us
and to our children? Were they kept so long out of habit and obscure
sentiment, as emblems of unspoken tenderness?

We might perhaps try to piece together a character just from the books
and papers left behind, or to restore our memories of our relative with
these old evidences of taste and interest—in fact we cannot help doing
so, in our nostalgic way—but there are too many lines of history here to
untangle—keepsakes, letters, bits of jewelry, and other belongings not
just of that one person but of other relatives and friends, accumulated
over a lifetime. What we sense here, beyond the individual personality,
is sheer humanness—desire, grief, hope, and dissatisfaction, the urge to
keep what is dear, to set up some defense against the obliterating snow
of time. In these things we glimpse our own inconsistencies and whims
and longings, and realize that we too are forever seeking certainty in the
perishing years.

But after enough hard experience we cannot believe that living comes to any wise conclusion by itself, or that suffering will finally be outlasted by patience alone. Among the numberless hours of dreaming and speculating, where is the true time that counts toward wisdom? Cause and effect crash through us every moment, unseen and unheard, perhaps, but making us and remaking us according to the nature of our actions. In considering history—of our own family or of all humanity—we are considering actions, changes, the endless turns of circumstance, the surge and fall of generations. Why should our own generation necessarily surge higher than any other and carry us with it? Whatever the fanfare around us, still we act as individuals, well or badly, and receive the results of those actions. Our own past and all of history teach us the essential sameness of worldly things, show us the prevailing passions of living beings, but do not direct us to liberation from suffering. For that we need the teaching of the Buddha.

We gaze out the window at the dazzling, motionless neighborhood—bright white under a winter blue—and though the near houses are new enough, time seems strangely indefinite, blown away as the snow has been blown away from the branches of trees. We might almost be living in any century, looking up with surprise from any life, any domestic moment, into that amazing emptiness of sky. Always it is something like this when we sit still enough and watch with mindfulness. We sense the vastness of the season, wherein we are always, it seems, beginning again to grapple with birth and death, beginning and hesitating and faltering for lack of knowledge or lack of faith.

Whether we yearn for the charming past or the intriguing future, still those white and blue depths of winter surround us—emblematic of the great *dukkha* that is continually regenerated out of ignorance by our actions. While cause and effect inexorably race on we have no grounds for esteeming ourselves necessarily superior or inferior, in moral safety or religious confidence, to past generations or our own past lives. We make our guesses, restrain or obey our impulses, and run along through the brief warmth of our years, hoping to attain at last to peace or contentment; but history, read out of books or sensed now in the belongings of our family, tells only of sameness beneath the flickering of incidents—the timeless moral questions and the groping for certainty.

Staring out the window while the old papers lie light on our fingers, we find we cannot patronize the past at all, cannot think it quaint and strange, when all the loves and fears that the papers hint at burn in us on this bright and desolate afternoon. Time falls off, blows away in the perception of deep kinship even apart from names and bloodlines. All those multitudes born to ponder and endure birth and death, and all those untraceable antecedents to our present cares—how near they seem, how familiar. Impermanence paradoxically draws us together, because each generation experiences these same sequences of birth, aging, and death; each questions the aching mysteries of change; each loves and hopes and cries in pain. Each single being, too, flies on from birth to birth, not as a self but as a pattern of conditions, with each life making the impetus for a new one here or there. It is not easy, the Buddha says, to find a living being who has not at some time been our own close relative; such is the inconceivable depth of *saṃsāra*, the succession of births and deaths. The string of our past lives, the string of impersonal causality that has brought about this present existence, runs back and back without beginning. Wherever we look, in whatever age or instant, suffering persists as an inescapable fact and challenge.

In such a flood of arising and passing away, how foolish is our trust in trivial novelty. Never mind the blaring of any generation—what is the noble life for a conscious being? Why should we not put our will into that? We are not separated from the mortal condition of our ancestors, and, wonderfully, we are not separated from the liberating Dhamma. The truths rediscovered by the Buddha are not, after all, lost behind a wall of centuries—they remain here, around us, accessible to the informed seeker. Where there is knowledge of Dhamma and where there is the will to contemplate the world that our senses show us, there is the possibility of weakening and destroying *dukkha* and attaining *Nibbāna*.

And if it is true, as it now seems, that no meaningful time separates us from all our sentient kin back through appalling ages of birth and death, why should we regard the Buddha himself as remote beyond all hoping? We are much given to exotic dreams, as if the great sages of the past existed only in some fantastic, unattainable land of magic; but the Buddha points to our immediate, individual responsibility: "One who sees the Dhamma sees me; one who sees me sees the Dhamma" (*Saṃyutta Nikāya* 22:87). No imagination will guarantee us that vision—only careful attention here and now will do that. The present moment is usually unexciting and ordinary, whatever the historical period—with the icy tedium of winter and the sweltering drone of summer, the work and the rest, the unclear longing for liberation—but if by study and by mindfulness we begin to see the Dhamma, even the first glimmer of its brilliance, we may be sure we are in the presence of the great teacher.

What then should we ask of the teacher? What do we expect of him? Do we hope to warm ourselves by his wisdom, marveling at his enlightenment as at some worldly spectacle? Only the development of our own character according to the Dhamma will bring us genuine peace. We will see no wonders as long as we make no effort to purify our minds. The Buddha says that even though a monk might hold on to the hem of his robe and follow right behind him, if he is still full of defilements and has not disciplined himself he would not, in truth, see the Buddha, because he fails to see the Dhamma. But there is, happily, another way of following:

> Bhikkhus, even though a bhikkhu might live a hundred leagues away, if he is not covetous for objects of desire, not strongly passionate, not malevolent, uncorrupt in thought, with mindfulness established, clearly comprehending, concentrated, of unified mind and controlled faculties, he is close to me and I am close to him. What is the reason? That bhikkhu sees Dhamma. Seeing Dhamma, he sees me.

(Itivuttaka 92)

Rightly seeing Dhamma, then, one should act according to Dhamma. A *Tathāgata*, a Buddha, is not someone who does our work for us; he is one who explains what we must do, and if we have not looked as he advises and have not begun to do the vital work, then we have missed his essential message. Cause and effect have driven us down this beginningless cataract of time, and if we are ever to cease tumbling or escape from the flood altogether we must eliminate the causes of harm and supply the causes of good. All ages tremble with covetousness, passion, malevolence, and corrupted thought; and for all ages and all persons protection can be found in mindfulness, concentration, and control of the sense faculties. These are powers we can develop and exercise, whatever the external circumstances may be.

For too long, perhaps, we have merely waited, expecting or hoping for some yet unrealized strength to spring up in us, or for our uncertainty to dissolve in a fortuitous onset of wisdom. We wish for a grand wind of inspiration to lift us suddenly from our gloom; but this wind is not summoned by mere desire. It is brought into being by conscious, faithful adherence to the Dhamma.

Now we sit in a still room full of sunlight and only imagine wind. Imagination is a beginning, perhaps, an adventure among possibilities— but we must do more. History enriches us, educates us with the panorama of strife and suffering and sometimes nobility, age upon countless age; and it stirs us, perhaps, to seek nobility, to seek liberation. We may with profit contemplate other lives gone before us, with their deeds of courage and friendship, their afflictions borne with grace; but the real character, the worth, of our own existence is determined by the acts we ourselves intend and carry out now. What do we perceive directly but these small occurrences of sight, sound, smell, taste, touch, and thought? These make the landscapes of our world and thus deserve our study. When we know without confusion exactly what conditions surround us or arise within our minds at any moment, we are prepared to act confidently and honorably.

What does surround us now? We sit breathing in a room full of our belongings and the belongings of our ancestors, a quiet room now blazing with tremendous sunlight from a window, through which we feel the paradoxical warmth of a freezing afternoon. Just outside the glass an icicle clings to the gutter, glimmering and flashing. We contemplate this small mystery of the silent, creative winter—just one more fragment of wonder, framed by empty blue. Despite the cold, the sun draws from the slender icicle slow, brilliant drops—small measures of passing time. How long will the icicle last, melting and freezing, filtering and reflecting

light? How long will the snow beyond endure? Or the neighborhood itself
with the streets and houses and trees we depend on to know our position
in the universe? Despite the apparent frozen stillness, the helpless motion
within things has not ceased—drops keep falling in tiny flashes—and
within this room dust floats and turns silently in the light between us and
the window. Wherever we look we find confirmation of what the Buddha
taught twenty-five centuries ago: "All formations are impermanent." And
we too, leaving our possessions, go on according to our actions, take shape
and lose shape like the icicle, through rebirth after rebirth. There is
nowhere any base for vanity, no reason to grasp at that which changes. By
slow drops, by rivulets and rivers, our actions, our true belongings, give
rise to good and evil. So if we see this should we not act mindfully in the
way of virtue so that the cause of suffering may be abandoned and the way
to freedom followed?

In the stillness we turn from the bright window to our papers and keepsakes again. We preside; we organize; but these belongings rest only temporarily in our custody. Our descendants will in their turn extract what
sentiment or meaning they can. We cannot hold these things forever, but
we might contemplate them in the light of Dhamma to learn our own true
condition and arouse energy for a worthy life. Here is a box of sewing
supplies, with spools and pins arrayed, and here are yards of fine cloth
never cut or sewn—like beautiful intentions never acted upon. Have we
yet carried through on our own best intentions or held off till inspiration
fell asleep again?

Here are more photographs of our relatives back through the decades.
And here is a good one of our grandfather as a young man. (We might
not have known him but for the name and the date written on the back.)
In our eternally childish way we are surprised that he could ever have
been young; but there indeed he sits at a picnic table in summer, relaxed
and smiling slightly. We admire the picture for a moment, sinking into
an ancient season—but now we pause, for we suddenly realize, in the
way the light and shadows lie there, that the sun on that unrecoverable
day eighty years gone is aflame before him. The sun blazes in his face,
warms his skin; and he in his smiling youth looks out at a chaos of time,
trying to see shapes clearly—as we do now, staring at the mystery of
our day. He is young here, lithe and brave but still overwhelmed by the

sun, wondering and guessing at the laws beneath the fires of nature, gathering his young ambitions, and waiting, it may be, for the inscrutable maturing of his strength. Where shall he travel? What adventure shall he seek? What hope shall guide him? We know some of this—incidents of biography, facts of place and time—and we remember something of his character in old age; but are we now, sitting on our little hill of years long after his life has closed, any bolder in action than this young man in his summer, any deeper in understanding, any surer in faith?

With the old photograph in our hands we turn again to the window, where light and mystery pour in upon us. It is our time to sound out the world, our time to decide which way to go. No longevity will carry us to truth, no applause of friends, no frenzy of accomplishment, no catalogue of honors gained. Our solitude on this winter day reminds us of our inescapable, individual responsibility for our own character, for our own decline or advancement. We lean toward the window; we look for peace under that blue stillness, across that sunlit snow; but neither our social hilarity nor our lonely desire has yet lifted us out of doubt and danger. Only wise action according to Dhamma can do that. And where is this Dhamma? Is it closed up in books, lost and mute in antiquity? Words remain only shadows until we ponder them with ardent will, until with whatever tender faith we can gather we totter out into the world and try to live by them. Then they begin to release whatever music they contain.

Now outside the window we see a couple of children staggering along the snowy sidewalk, pulling sleds, panting cheerfully. They stop for a moment, and we hear their shrill voices faintly through the glass. They laugh and grin, gesticulating extravagantly; then they plunge onward until they pass out of our view, sending a slow wave across our imagination. We look after them, smiling, seeing in them resurgent strength and hope; but they are already gone in the brilliance of the low sun. All generations pass thus, riding the vehicle of their deeds, not guaranteed peace by nature but free to win it. Ancestors known and unknown, strangers and friends, all beings sailing in *saṃsāra's* gale—let us wish them safe progress; and let us, while any strength still breathes in us, win what we can of timeless peace.

Our names will be memories, our belongings the curious inheritance of wondering children, but for now the sun still blazes and the dimensions of the world can be known. We have this capable breath and the icicle on the gutter and the landscape before our senses. And we have the good Dhamma, the ageless, shining inheritance for living, hoping beings. By *this* warmth we may survive the winter, by *this* light find the certainty we need.

16
ACROSS THE FRAGRANT FIELD

The teaching of the Buddha gives us the means to live by wise purpose in the midst of haphazard nature. It may be that if we apply enough skill and energy to mundane matters of making a living and protecting our property we can prosper—as the world sees it—but we can never through material prosperity alone secure any deep peace or freedom. Growing up, approaching maturity as human beings, means, at the least, understanding the necessity to honor and to live by noble standards. When the Buddha at last attained supreme enlightenment he reflected, "One dwells in suffering if one is without reverence and deference" (*Saṃyutta Nikāya* 6:2), and he himself determined to honor the magnificent Dhamma he had discovered.

It is our human nature to seek for and to depend on ideals of purpose and conduct, but it is not enough to select just *any* ideal or to settle on a purpose no grander than the achievement of fame and sensual gratification. Rather we must, by listening, studying, considering, and observing, find that which promises to be of consistent, universal benefit. Once we have discovered such an ideal, we cannot treat it as a distant abstraction, revering it only in theory, but must set about living in accordance with it, showing our respect through action. Nature forever dances on in inconclusive patterns, taking no account of the happiness of any lone creature; but the Buddha teaches for the benefit of all, pointing out those pure and virtuous patterns that, through the natural working of cause and effect, culminate in perfect happiness. If we are inspired by his teaching, if we see its beauty and logic, we must see also that, however difficult it seems, it is meant for our good and can be followed in this age or any age. Then we are left to decide what we, as free beings, are going to do about it.

Our trying winters will subside like all things, but whether the summers that follow will blossom with any real gladness depends on how intently we live by Dhamma. What are these garden fragrances and these wonders of clouds but more formations that cannot be held, that entertain and depart, that give no ultimate security? We say it is summer now, an epoch of ease and recreation, but is it also a summer of wise purpose and wise action, yielding good fruit? How long shall we wait for the world to perfect itself while we sink in dreams? If we idle through our seasons we will get no relief from affliction, and time, meanwhile, will press upon us and eventually break down all our indolent comforts. If, however, our ideals are noble, and if we act with good will and faith, we will find more than momentary flowers and will not have to fear the inevitable rearrangement of the world.

Across our neighborhood today legions of tiny seeds wrapped in white fluff are blowing, adding more clouds to the clouds of summer. So shall we walk out, as we have walked before, not just to enjoy the moist breeze from the woods, but to refresh ourselves with useful knowledge? Should we not, whether in leisure or on a determined errand, establish mindfulness and see what it will show us? All around us the Dhamma is manifest, available for our examination, and when we have well absorbed doctrine and considered it at length we can make use of the thousand expressions of reality we encounter to inspire us and strengthen us.

It is summer, a season for slow walking, for long contemplation of the shade and sunlight that variously fall upon us. Everywhere in our neighborhood, it seems, crickets are singing, making a shrill, monotonous music. Let us wander about today in a free hour, out in a field where the grass is thick. We find that our anxious steps are restrained, slowed, and disciplined by the bristling stalks and stems and leaves; and our thoughts, which otherwise might wander through the clouds, are forced down to the rank earth, down to the work we have to do to make our way across the field. Where are the briars that will catch at us? How long or short a step will serve right here? This season's growth fortunately is not too thick to stop us, only dense enough to make us more careful, more deliberate, and thus more conscious of what is happening. Here the Dhamma of remembered words takes on the freshness of unmowed grass.

Are we still impatient, eager to be moving in a straight line toward some tree or rock or house—as if everything of interest and importance must exist somewhere other than here? Why should we hurry at the call of a desire? Do we step into a field only to cross it and find again more immensities beyond still uncomprehended? Here, where we stand and turn, is a universe of moths and clover, where bees glide, where crickets scamper and hide, where life and death revolve under our gaze. Out of the winter all of this intensity comes to be, and into the winter it falls again. If our human world is to be accounted superior, in what does that superiority lie? We too are mortal; we wince at thorns; but we retain the power to contemplate, to conceive of a good beyond the hour's diversion, and to bring something of that good into being by our deeds.

Why should we always be crying for the sunshine and then squandering it and crying for its return? Flowers *might* be more plentiful, more beautiful in another corner of the meadow, but to seek always for newer, more elaborate sensations while the fair day fades can hardly be wise. It would surely be better to find our ideal wherever we stand and to work for the arising of the good—because, even during delightful weather, *dukkha* persists. This ideal, this Dhamma we learn and then recognize all about us, is what can confront and defeat *dukkha*.

We see these parks, fields, and woods as beautiful, as antidotes to our anxiety, but we ought not to search them for aesthetic pleasure alone and miss their urgent illustration of *dukkha*. The small, vulnerable creatures whose songs and dances we enjoy fly on toward winters without wisdom, toward summers in bondage to ignorance, while we—no less mortal, no less subject to pain—have heard something of the Dhamma and pause now in our lovely summer, considering whether we must fly likewise through cycles of *dukkha*. This is our real advantage: the possibility of perceiving and pursuing truth—not mere longevity or strength. Looming over the crickets and the butterflies, we reflect on our own frailties and on the Dhamma that is our priceless human inheritance. Shall we go on through our fortunate hours gazing and admiring only, never acting with confidence?

Soon after the Buddha reached full enlightenment he decided to teach the Dhamma, perceiving that there were those in the world who could understand this liberating truth if they heard it. If we hear, and if we begin to see how his words so wisely describe and explain our daily experience, we will perhaps be moved to conduct ourselves in body, speech, and mind in the way he taught. Conditions fly loose everywhere, like these million seeds swirling in the careless wind; and conditions undirected, uncontrolled, give rise to mortality and sorrow endlessly. But wholesome conditions deliberately brought together—actions done in the direction of Dhamma—give rise to greater welfare for living beings. The Buddha opened the gates to liberation, to the deathless *Nibbāna*, by teaching this Dhamma, showing this path, and encouraging long-bewildered seekers of the good to seek it here.

This field today smells sweet; the briars are manageable; yellow butterflies race around us; and at each slow step of ours grasshoppers and other tiny creatures pop off their perches to either side. We hear all around, at different distances, the chattering of insects and birds—nothing especially enchanting, only imperfect suggestions of beauty. We walk along, considering these perceptions, noticing how they overlie one another, building a world up for a moment's contemplation. We remember the ravaging winter, think of the next one not so far away, and ponder the impermanence of this moment of sunshine. Our steps, we now know, must be more careful, strong, and sure—not precipitate or hasty but aimed deliberately at the good.

We do not, it may be, see very far in the hot air of this summer day. And we do not, it may be, perceive with unshakable certainty the truth of the Dhamma. But assuredly our senses tell us how causes flame up in every moment, how friendliness and generosity beautify the mind, how restraint of the unworthy thought makes room for what is worthy. Reflecting on this much knowledge, and looking deeper with the Buddha's guidance, we gain the faith to venture onward in the right direction. It is not a matter, after all, of finding meadows still more flowery than this one but of forsaking all self-made folly wherever we walk.

Around us countless delicate seeds are blowing—tiny clouds adrift in vast currents—and above them the greater clouds roll under sun and unseen stars and inconceivable levels of being. How we have drifted, too, through many dizzy years! But now we begin to find vital truths within these summer sensations. This body will carry us a little further, surely. These good aspirations will move us toward honorable efforts.

The sun burns down on the wide green field, and we begin to get a little too warm, so at length, being reminded anew of impermanence, we set off without haste toward our home, our duties, and other scenes of contemplation. Across the fragrant field, then under great trees, and on down the sidewalks of our neighborhood we go through unmeasured immensities of time, our feet falling steadily on the earth.

As we walk from block to block many facts and symbols rise up before us. So many signs display the truth. We get a little tired on our way, it is true, but to whom would we complain? All living beings, like us, are sailing on the wind of their own actions. We see children trotting about on these lawns with cheerful innocence, while their parents, though weighted with their own sorrows, wave at us and call a greeting. We smile and wave back at them, and our course through time grows a little steadier. The power of our own action, most wonderfully, can remake us into what we choose. Everywhere around us, whether understood or not, causes go on rolling the seasons, and causes swell to grief or gladness for every creature.

Once in the snow we looked about longingly for a path and saw only hints in nature's solemn motions, but now in a summer that vanishes just as surely we discover we have been living all along among brilliant markers. The Buddha's teachings have reached us now; the singing of crickets has reached us; and our senses become alert to wonder. Whatever the reckless skies and earth may do, it is virtue that calls up the finest season, concentration that brings the sun on our soil, and wisdom that perfects the noblest fruit.

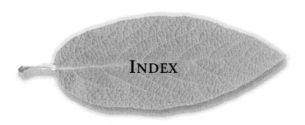

INDEX

T

V

W

WISDOM PUBLICATIONS

Wisdom Publications, a not-for-profit publisher, is dedicated to making available authentic Buddhist works for the benefit of all. We publish translations of the sutras and tantras, commentaries and teachings of past and contemporary Buddhist masters, and original works by the world's leading Buddhist scholars. We publish our titles with the appreciation of Buddhism as a living philosophy and with the special commitment to preserve and transmit important works from all the major Buddhist traditions.

To learn more about Wisdom, or to browse books online, visit our website at wisdompubs.org. You may request a copy of our mail-order catalog online or by writing to:

Wisdom Publications
199 Elm Street
Somerville, Massachusetts 02144 USA
Telephone: (617) 776-7416
Fax: (617) 776-7841
Email: info@wisdompubs.org
www.wisdompubs.org

The Wisdom Trust

As a not-for-profit publisher, Wisdom is dedicated to the publication of fine Dharma books for the benefit of all sentient beings and dependent upon the kindness and generosity of sponsors in order to do so. If you would like to make a donation to Wisdom, please do so through our Somerville office. If you would like to sponsor the publication of a book, please write or email us at the address above.

Thank you.